Journal of Prisoners
on Prisons

... allowing our experiences and analysis to be added to the forum that will constitute public opinion could help halt the disastrous trend toward building more fortresses of fear which will become in the 21ˢᵗ century this generation's monuments to failure.

Jo-Ann Mayhew (1988)

Volume 32
Number 2
2023

JOURNAL OF PRISONERS ON PRISONS

EDITORIAL STAFF:

Editors:	Justin Piché	Dialogue Editor:	Olivia Gemma
	Kevin Walby	Prisoners' Struggles Editor:	Vicki Chartrand
Editorial Assistants:	Zimo Meng	Book Review Editor:	Melissa Munn
	Nicole Necsefor	Online Production Editor:	Victoria Morris
Issue Editors:	Kevin Walby and Justin Piché		

The *Journal of Prisoners on Prisons* publishes two issues a year. Its purpose is to encourage research on a wide range of issues related to crime, justice, and punishment by current and former prisoners. Donations to the JPP are welcomed.

SUBMISSIONS: Current and former prisoners are encouraged to submit original papers, collaborative essays, discussions transcribed from tape, book reviews, and photo or graphic essays that have not been published elsewhere. The *Journal* does not usually publish fiction or poetry. The *Journal* will publish articles in either French or English. Articles should be no longer than 20 pages typed and double-spaced or legibly handwritten. Electronic submissions are gratefully received. Writers may elect to write anonymously or under a pseudonym. For references cited in an article, the writer should attempt to provide the necessary bibliographic information. Refer to the references cited in this issue for examples. Submissions are reviewed by members of the Editorial Board. Selected articles are corrected for composition and returned to the authors for their approval before publication. Papers not selected are returned with editorial comments. Revised papers may be resubmitted. Please submit bibliographical and contact information, to be published alongside articles unless otherwise indicated.

SUBSCRIPTIONS, SUBMISSIONS AND ALL OTHER CORRESPONDENCE:

Journal of Prisoners on Prisons
c/o Justin Piché, PhD
Department of Criminology, University of Ottawa
Ottawa, Ontario, Canada K1N 6N5

e-mail: jpp@uottawa.ca
website: www.jpp.org

SUBCRIPTIONS:	One Year	Two Years	Three Years
Incarcerated Subscribers	$30.00	$50.00	$60.00
Non-incarcerated Subscribers	$40.00	$70.00	$90.00
Prison Libraries & Schools, Libraries & Institutions	$60.00	$110.00	$150.00

Subscriptions by mail are payable in Canadian or American dollars. In Canada, 5% HST must be added to all orders. We encourage subscription purchases online at https://press.uottawa.ca/en/journal-of-prisoners-on-prisons/

BACK ISSUES:
Each back issue is $20 and each back double-issue is $35 (Canadian dollars) + shipping costs. In Canada, 5% HST must be added to all orders. Back issues can be purchased from the University of Ottawa Press at https://press.uottawa.ca/en/search-results/?keyword=Journal+of+Prisoners+on+Prisons. If interested in obtaining issues that are out of print, please contact the JPP directly. Further information regarding course orders and distribution can be obtained from the University of Ottawa Press at:

University of Ottawa Press	phone:	1-613-562-5246	email: puo-uop@uottawa.ca
542 King Edward Avenue	fax:	1-613-562-5247	website: www.press.uottawa.ca
Ottawa, Ontario, Canada K1N 6N5			

Co-published by the University of Ottawa Press and the Journal of Prisoners on Prisons.

Printed and Bound in Canada

ISSN 0838-164X (print) | 2816-7570 (online)
ISBN 978-0-7766-4029-7 (print) | 978-0-7766-4030-3 (online)

In This Issue

DEDICATION

The Life and Work of Sarah Speight
Justin Piché

I first met Sarah in the spring of 2018 when she was looking to get involved in a group that began its work over a decade ago called the Criminalization and Punishment Education Project, which aims to reduce the use and harms of policing and imprisonment, as well as build safer communities through research on and advocacy for alternatives. At the time, Sarah was new to Ottawa and, with a background of research and advocacy on overdose prevention sites, she was looking to get involved in community organizing to work in solidarity with people who struggle to meet their basic needs and, in the process, enhance our collective well-being and safety.

Early conversations with Sarah led to the creation of the Jail Accountability & Information Line in December 2018. Sarah played a key role in launching this initiative and running the hotline that took thousands of calls from people imprisoned at the Ottawa-Carleton Detention Centre in its early years. Through this initiative, Sarah worked with imprisoned people on various human rights and re-entry issues they faced, including getting access to medical care behind and beyond bars. For instance, I recall the early days of the hotline where Sarah literally spent days advocating for a person who had fallen off the bunk in their jail cell to the concrete floor and broke their leg to get transferred to a hospital so that he could get examined and get access the care he needed that was being denied by jail staff and management who did not believe him. I also recall numerous instances where Sarah arranged for doctor's appointments for people coming out of the jail to ensure that their opioid substitution prescriptions would continue once they were released so that they would not turn to street drugs, and potentially overdose and die. There is no doubt Sarah saved lives that through her community organizing and advocacy.

In 2019, Sarah became Dialogue Editor for the *Journal of Prisoners on Prisons*, which is a section aimed at bringing various people with lived expertise of imprisonment in conversation with each other to advance thought and praxis on a particular challenge facing prisoners. Among the contributions Sarah made in this role was the publication of Volume 28, Number 2 of the journal featuring a dialogue on "Prison (In)justice in Canada at the Crossroads", which served as a clarion call for changes to federal imprisonment in the country that remain needed.

By 2019, Sarah had also been fast-tracked through the Master's program in geography at the University of Ottawa to the doctoral program. It is at that point that I, along with geographer Eric Crighton, became her co-supervisors. Of all my doctoral supervisions, I was most excited to be involved in Sarah's project that brought into conversation insights from human geography, socio-legal studies, and critical criminology to make sense of how so few reforms following deaths in custody and related coroner's inquests in Ontario result in meaningful reductions in people dying behind bars. At a time when preventable deaths in custody continue to occur, her study drew on observations and transcripts of coroner's inquest hearings, findings and recommendations, interviews with coroners, crown attorneys and lawyers representing inquest intervenors, as well as news coverage, to generate knowledge on the forces that limit the scope and actors that have standing in these cases and, by connection, how these constraints can lead to inadequate recommendations and barriers to their implementation. In so doing, her doctoral thesis had already impacted policies and procedures for coroner's inquests related to deaths in custody in Ontario that, at least in some cases, extended the gaze of such proceedings beyond jail and prison walls, producing recommendations in the fields of health, mental health, policing, and other human services that could, if implemented, prevent deaths in custody by diverting people away from criminalization and incarceration, particularly those living with mental health and drug use issues. Sarah had completed five of eight of her doctoral dissertation chapters, with three others well underway. She was set to complete and defend her doctoral thesis in September 2023. It is absolutely heartbreaking that Sarah will not finish what I and many others, including researchers and those involved in coroner's inquests, considered to be ground-breaking work.

Sarah had plans to continue this work either as a postdoctoral fellow or professor. Drawing on Political Activist Ethnography, including interviews with supervising coroners and forensic pathologists, formal and informal information requests with death investigation bodies, and discussion groups with people impacted by policing and prison deaths across Canada, Sarah next wanted to explore how death investigations are undertaken, the barriers faced by those seeking information on carceral deaths, and how to ethically manage such information in ways that do not deepen the trauma of people who have lost loved ones in the context of policing and imprisonment. What Sarah had envisioned as her next project was both original and significant as it sought to generate information 'from above' (through research with actors that steer carceral death investigations) and 'from below' (through research with the loved ones and communities impacted by these preventable tragedies) to inform how we understand policing and prison deaths, and the possibilities for transparency and action in their wake. This is critical and much needed work to be undertaken at a time when people continue to die in custody. And, again, I am heartbroken that Sarah is not alive to see her vision through.

While Sarah is no longer with us, she nonetheless has left us with a rich legacy, which can be felt and seen in various ways. For instance, Sarah published several works over the years, including an academic journal issue, a book chapter, a journal article, seven reports, and seven op-eds with by-lines in the *Ottawa Citizen*, *The Globe and Mail* and *The Conversation*. Her thoughts will live on, but most importantly the impact she had on all of us will stay in our hearts forever.

As a professor, as someone who supervises the research of graduate students, you understand that they will come and go, that they will start and complete their degrees or sometimes not, and move on to other things, whether inside or outside academia. In rare cases, you forge collaborations and friendships you hope will last a lifetime. That is what I and several other professors had with Sarah.

The last time I saw Sarah was three days before she died. We had a meeting in my office. We made plans for the completion of her remaining doctoral thesis chapters and for a research assistantship this summer. I did not know then, but I know now that when Sarah walked out of my office that Wednesday, she also exited my life before we could finish what we sought to accomplish together – before she could see through everything she had planned to do. We have all lost someone who was absolutely brilliant, who was a hard worker, who was incredibly caring and always put others before herself. It is a tremendous loss. This has been difficult to process.

To Sarah's family and friends, I am sorry for your loss. I hope that with time that our grief about Sarah's death can give way to peace in our minds and hearts. Do take care.

SELECTED CONTRIBUTIONS
BY SARAH SPEIGHT

Peer-Reviewed Publications

Speight, Sarah, Jarrod Shook, Justin Piché and Kevin Walby (2020) Special Issue: Prison (In)justice in Canada at a Crossroads, *Journal of Prisoners on Prisons*, 28(2): 1-194.

Benslimane, Aisha, Sarah Speight, Justin Piché and Aaron Doyle (2020) "The Jail Accountability & Information Line: Early Reflections on Praxis", *Journal of Law and Social Policy*, 33: 111-133.

Piché, Justin, Sarah Speight and Kevin Walby (2022) "The Prison in/ as a Pandemic: Human Rights Implications of Carceral 'Solutions' in Response to COVID-19 in Canada", in Alex Neve (ed.), *2021 Canadian Yearbook of Human Rights*, Ottawa: Human Rights Research and Education Centre, pp. 134-141.

Reports

Speight, Sarah, Aisha Benslimane, Aaron Doyle and Justin Piché (2019) *Monthly Evaluation – Report #1*, JAIL / Jail Accountability & Information Line brief submitted to the Ottawa-Carleton Detention Centre and the Ontario Ministry of Community Safety and Correctional Services – January.

Speight, Sarah, Aisha Benslimane, Aaron Doyle and Justin Piché (2019) *Quarterly Advocacy Report #1*, JAIL / Jail Accountability & Information Line brief submitted to the Ottawa-Carleton Detention Centre and the Ontario Ministry of Community Safety and Correctional Services – March.

Speight, Sarah, Aisha Benslimane, Lydia Dobson, Aaron Doyle and Justin Piché (2019) *Quarterly Advocacy Report #2*, JAIL / Jail Accountability & Information Line brief submitted to the Ottawa-Carleton Detention Centre and the Ontario Ministry of the Solicitor General – August.

Benslimane, Aisha, Justin Piché, Sarah Speight, Lydia Dobson, Aaron Doyle (2019) *Will You Accept the Charges? The Case for the Government of Ontario to Move Away from the Prohibitive, Predatory, and Outdated Telephone System in its Provincial Jails and Towards Accessible, Free Calling That Promotes Connections Essential to Community Well-being and Safety*, JAIL / Jail Accountability & Information Line report submitted to the Ontario Ministry of the Solicitor General – October.

Speight, Sarah, Aisha Benslimane, Aaron Doyle and Justin Piché (2019) *Quarterly Report #3*, JAIL / Jail Accountability & Information Line brief submitted to the Ottawa-Carleton Detention Centre and the Ontario Ministry of the Solicitor General – December.

Benslimane, Aisha, Lydia Dobson, Sabine Seeman, Steph Rychlo, Aaron Doyle, Justin Piché and Sarah Speight (2021) *Inadequate Complaints Procedures at the Ottawa Jail and Recommendations for Change*, JAIL / Jail Accountability & Information Line report submitted to the Ottawa-Carleton Detention Centre and the Ontario Ministry of the Solicitor General – August.

Speight, Sarah and Alex McClelland (2022) *Ontario Deaths in Custody on the Rise*, Tracking (In)Justice Project – December.

Op-eds

Speight, Sarah, Aisha Benslimane, Aaron Doyle and Justin Piché (2018) "Stop jailing people with mental health issues. It kills", *Ottawa Citizen* – December 9.

Speight, Sarah, Aisha Benslimane, Aaron Doyle and Justin Piché (2019) "Ontario must address urgent health issues at Ottawa jail", *Ottawa Citizen* – January 25.

Leblanc, Sean, Sarah Speight, Justin Piché and Aisha Benslimane (2019) "Ontario needs to reduce overdose risks behind and beyond bars", *Ottawa Citizen* – April 8.

Speight, Sarah, Aisha Benslimane and Justin Piché (2020) "A just transition: Moving away from prison construction in Canada", *Canadian Association for Refugee and Forced Migration Studies Blog* – February 14.

Speight, Sarah (2020) "Canadian penitentiaries: Dangerous for aging and palliative prisoners", *The Conversation* – March 3.

Piché, Justin and Sarah Speight (2020) "Build communities, not cages: Jails are death traps, no matter how new", *Globe and Mail* – October 24.

Speight, Sarah and Justin Piché (2021) "Ion scanner rollout in provincial jails: Expensive, ineffective and harmful", *Ottawa Citizen* – February 17.

ABOUT THE AUTHOR

Justin Piché, PhD is Associate Professor in the Department of Criminology and Director of the Carceral Studies Research Collective at the University of Ottawa. He is also a member of the Criminalization and Punishment Education Project and Co-editor of the *Journal of Prisoners on Prisons*. During the COVID-19 pandemic, he has been tracking coronavirus infections and measures in Canadian jails, prisons, and penitentiaries as part of the Prison Pandemic Partnership.

INTRODUCTION FROM THE ISSUE EDITORS

From Systems of Abuse to Circles of Care
Kevin Walby and Justin Piché

One place to look for the damage that prisons and the criminal justice system cause in our world is the hospital. Specifically, intensive care units (ICUs) are places where the obvious harms of carceral spaces and criminal justice practices show up on the bodies of so many people. The following are stories relayed to the first author by ICU nurses in Canada. Recently, two guards from a jail accompanied a prisoner who was suffering from a severe allergic reaction of unknown origins to the intensive care unit. The prisoner was shackled to the bed and restrained, while guards lurked over his semiconscious body. The nurses attempting to begin care asked the guards for the man's baseline. A baseline is a set of figures representing someone's health. It could include blood pressure and other figures. When asked for his baseline, the guards responded, "His baseline? Idiot". This gives the reader clear insight into how some guards think about imprisoned people, as well as their health and their well-being. Instead of conveying some kind of useful information to assist with the person's health and treatment, the guards simply stood there vigilantly, intermittently reporting back to their superior at the jail.

A more tragic story happened a few months earlier. A prisoner was transported from a different jail. The prisoner was totally unconscious and was bleeding from several orifices. The emergency room doctors thought that due to the loss of blood the prisoner patient required a transfusion, which they did perform before sending him to the intensive care unit. When arriving at the ICU, the patient was sent for several scans. It was found that there was incredible damage done to the internal organs of the prisoner. Catastrophic damage was done to the intestines of the patient. Once again, two guards stood coldly and silently in the room. When the nurses explained to the guards that they had to call the family due to the catastrophic nature of the injuries, the guards protested and said that could not happen. The nurses resisted and called the family members to the hospital. When the family members arrived, the guards prevented the family from entering the room citing security concerns. The nurses explained again to the guards that the prisoner had suffered catastrophic organ damage to the extent that he was bleeding from all orifices and his death was imminent. The guards continued to protest and called their supervisor at the jail. The nurses again pushed back and told the guards to leave the family members alone. The family members started to enter the room. This was an Indigenous man and it was important for the family to be there if the man was about to pass and enter into the spirit realm. The guards started to collect personal information from all persons entering the room, as if the persons in the room were security threats simply for wanting to be close to their family member as he was passing. The guards shared all that information with their supervisor. The prisoner suffered some brutal and sustained beating behind bars, and instead of showing some kind of care or concern, the guards simply displayed callous, merciless characteristics too often seen in carceral spaces and criminal justice practices.

A few months before that, a man who had been in an argument with his wife was agitated in front of his home, pacing back and forth on the sidewalk in the neighbourhood. Someone had called the police to respond to the scene. The police arrived and fairly soon after, upon further escalating the situation, attempted to restrain the man and tasered him several times in the chest. When this man arrived unconscious at the intensive care unit, he had severe burns on his skin, white and black charring, and destruction of the tissue on his upper torso. His heart had stopped due to the tasering. Not a single police officer performed CPR prior to paramedics arriving. The police continued to guard the man during treatment in the ICU as nurses and doctors attempted to resuscitate him, as they insisted he remained shackled to the bed as to them he was a suspect. The man could not be resuscitated as too much time had passed without CPR being administered since his cardiac arrest. Once again, a lack of care or concern by criminal justice personnel, even in the aftermath of harm directly caused by criminal justice personnel, can be observed.

Time and time again, the criminal justice system responds to transgression and everyday life with violence and adds harm to the equation. These kinds of scenes in intensive care units and emergency rooms are so prevalent that there are now doctors and nurses in the United States and in Canada that explicitly identify as penal abolitionists or carceral abolitionists (Paynter et al., 2022; DiZoglio and Telma, 2022). They have formed organizations to reveal that one of the main sources of harm to the bodies of the people they see in hospitals are police officers and prison guards. What kind of a society would continue to fund such an egregious form of harm that our most intelligent and most caring people (doctors and nurses) have explicitly flagged as destructive? What kind of a society would continue to promote that harm? Given such examples, what kinds of myths are necessary to sustain the idea that police and prisons promote order or safety and security in our world?

These scenes, which are just a few vignettes that could be drawn from any ICU in a major city from across Canada or the United States, point to a society whose priorities have been hijacked by powerful political interests such as police and guard unions (Ben-Moshe, 2020; Wang, 2018; Weaver and Lerman, 2010). There are so many forms of abuse, neglect, and harm that the criminal justice system causes in our world (Laniyonu, 2022; Skinns and Wooff, 2021; Harkin, 2015; Hancock and Jewkes, 2011). Carceral spaces are designed to deprive, maim, and dehumanize (Moran et al., 2018; Moran, 2012). There are many stories of people surviving detention, people surviving imprisonment, and people surviving criminal justice system surveillance too. The *Journal of Prisoners on Prisons* (JPP) exists to give voice to those survivors of system contact with criminal justice agencies, of the pains of policing and imprisonment, of the injustices of the so-called justice system, as well as the crimmigration control system and other parallel systems of control.

THIS ISSUE

In this issue of the *JPP*, we continue in this tradition of examining the multitude of harms caused by the criminal justice system in general, and prisons and jails in particular.

"Illusion of Parole" by Gordon Pack explores some of the problems with existing parole systems. Through an analysis of his experience of the Maryland Parole Commission, the author examines its history of biased and prejudiced choices, anomalies, and contradictions. He contends that the pains of incarceration continue throughout the parole commission process and when living on parole.

In "Belgian Prison Policy: Half a Century of Broken Promises" by Luk Vervaet, the author examines some of the contradictions of the criminal justice system and the harms that these contradictions cause in Belgium through an analysis of prison policy at a site of confinement called the Begijnenstraat. The Begijnenstraat was known decades ago to be an overcrowded, harmful facility that did not live up to the promises of the so-called rehabilitation of the penal state. The author shows that decades after recommendations were made, from 2018 to 2021 a series of journalistic inquiries showed that the health conditions inside the prison continued to be harmful. They also noted that there were pests, mice, and mold in the facility. The author suggests there is no reason to continue to put people in harm's way inside this facility.

In "CSC's Corporate Culture is the Fundamental Problem" by George Fraser, the author argues that CSC has a blue wall culture which promotes secrecy and allows harm to continue unabated behind bars. He further argues that the administration of CSC is largely out of touch regarding what happens on a day-to-day basis behind bars. In Canadian federal penitentiaries, he argues that corporate culture promotes a situation where carceral administrators and bureaucrats try to insulate or isolate themselves from culpability and jeopardy regarding all of the harms that do happen inside. As a result of this blue wall culture, human rights abuses are rampant within Canadian prisons. The author suggests that CSC as an organization has existed and has been doing things in such a poor way for so long that it will be incredibly difficult to change this corporate culture through anything like a standing committee or any of the pithy accountability mechanisms we have within the federal penitentiary system.

In "Restoring Our Honor from Gangs to Garrison", Shon Pernice suggests that prison life is marked by a lot of complex emotions from anger to hate, to resentment, to sadness, and that sometimes prisoners let these emotions get the best of them. However, these emotions can also be harnessed into a form of survival that allows prisoners to focus on the life ahead of them and doing good things in the world.

In "Changing Directions" by Darris Drake Jr., the author focuses on the future and change. More specifically, he writes about how he used to get wrapped up in the hate and the resentment – powerful and complex emotions that the prison in fact fostered. However, the author had to find a way to change to survive prison, and started to take part in education to overcome the inhumane conditions of carceral settings.

In "A Look at Prison Overcrowding from the Inside" by David Fleenor, the author looks at the problems with corrections in Oklahoma. Through examining the extent of prison overcrowding drawing both from official statistics and from his own experiences, the author also makes policy recommendations including a recommendation that the parole board hire formerly incarcerated persons as liaisons to help communication in the pardon and parole hearing setting. Academic research has long shown that the parole process can be arduous, stressful, and almost impossible for prisoners to overcome (Silverstein, 2001).

In "Reflecting on the Delivery of the Inside-Out Prison Exchange Program during COVID-19 Pandemic" by Dwayne Antojado, Haozhou Sun and Marietta Martinovic, the authors look at prison education involving inside students studying university courses with outside students. Outside students typically come into the prison to learn in that setting, and the inside-out process can often be transformational for all students. In Canada, this program is called Walls to Bridges (see Pollack and Mayor, 2023). Antojado and colleagues reflect on some of the challenges of prison education during the COVID-19 pandemic, arguing that many of the aims were still met by participants and organizers of the program. Prison education can be a very important confirmation of life for everyone involved and can help people survive prison. As an aside, it is important for scholars and teachers to push for access to education within prisons and jails given that it can be a powerful form of connection and learning and meaning for everyone involved.

In "An Ethnography of a Corrections Education Instructor: Critical Issues" by Robert Elton, the author argues that there are many challenges for people involved in prison education, including time and opportunity, lack of resources, and some of the challenging mental states that arise in a harmful setting such as the prison. As the article illustrates, there are many forms of peer pressure and challenges that people have to face inside such as limited access to simple technology that people on the outside take for granted, which are fairly instrumental in learning in the 21st century. The author suggests if educators and prisons are serious about prison education, they need to not only try to offer some classes, but they need to try to overcome these barriers and these forms of digital discrimination as well.

In "The Second Coming (Out)", Matthew Feeney writes about some of the challenges of being stereotyped and stigmatized within the prison and how people accused of any kind of sexual transgression are often treated heinously behind bars, not only by staff but by other imprisoned people. He argues that his whole experience of policing, being charged, detention, imprisonment, and trying to survive in the carceral setting as an extremely homophobic process, which has been damaging and traumatic.

In "Gender Not Fit For Prisons: On the Incompatibility of Gender as a Means to Segregate Prisoners", Dwayne Antojado examines the way that gender segregation occurs in prisons and jails, and the problems this and gender binaries present to persons who experience fluid gender or transgender identity. The author argues that most typical understandings of sex and gender rely on a binary of man or woman or male or female. Persons with gender fluidity, non-binary gender identities, or transgender identities are forced to navigate the criminal justice system and the gender binary system that is superimposed on it in ways that create many harms for their mental and physical well-being. There is what the author calls structural transphobia in prisons, and there is transgenderism and transphobia throughout the criminal justice system. This paper also examines the lack of transgender-specific policies, programming, and housing within carceral settings.

This issue also offers additional content as well, including a *Response* entitled "Moving Beyond the Prison Pandemic". The piece documents an event that took place in early-March involving people impacted by the punitive injustice system who shared their insights and expertise regarding the impact of COVID-19 on incarceration and community re-entry during the pandemic in Canada.

The *Prisoners' Struggles* section for this issue features three pieces documenting barriers to rehabilitation and re-entry. In "Agenda: Broken Corrections", Ken (Salamander) Hammond argues that in the Canadian context there are many contradictions and anomalies that mark the Correctional Service of Canada's approach to imprisonment. Writing as an Indigenous man who has spent dozens of years behind bars, the author writes about his experience of many forms of neglect during his time inside and the way that this mirrors broader colonial forms of control and neglect in Canada. In "Natural Life", Steven King Ainsworth argues that laws regarding sentence length and alternative sentences show a lack of humanity and care. The sentences for prisoners for serious felonies are excessive and do nothing to make society safer – they simply punish for the sake of it. The author looks at the state of California where thousands upon thousands of prisoners are doing many more years behind bars than would be fathomable or conceivable in any other purportedly democratic country in the world. In "Impartiality is a Fundamental and Legal Obligation of the Oklahoma Pardon and Parole Board", David Fleenor observes how the duty of the board to be impartial when assessing the evidence presented to them for pardons and parole is not evident in practice. The author documents cases where the board seems to display bias and even prejudice against persons with certain kinds of transgressions.

There are also a number of critical and engaging book reviews in this issue. These book reviews address a range of topics from wrongful conviction, to solitary confinement, to restorative justice, to lawbreaking and transgression, to carceral practices in the 21st century, and the lack of humanity in prisons and jails.

This collection of works authored or co-authored by criminalized people is book-ended with artwork created by Peter Collins in 2011 entitled "E.P.I.C" (End the Prison Industrial Complex) and "i-chain". We selected this artwork to underscore the continued need to resist and build alternatives to carceral control, including in pandemic times where the reach of penality continues to expand in communities through the growth of technologies such as electronic monitoring (see, for example, Kilgore and Dolinar, 2023).

This general issue marks the completion of the thirty-second volume of the *Journal of Prisoners on Prisons*, which we dedicate to Sarah Speight, who was the journal's Dialogue Editor from 2019 until her sudden death in mid-March 2023. As we note in the *Dedication* preceding this introduction, Sarah was a valued member of our team whose presence and contributions aimed at abolishing deadly criminalization and incarceration policies, practices, and institutions will be greatly missed.

In closing, thank you to all the authors who have contributed their experiences, however painful, to the pages of *JPP*. It takes great courage to write about injustice. Oftentimes, prisoner writers communicate their views at great risk to themselves and at risk of reprimand from guards and prison administrators. Education should be a human right that goes along with freedom of expression. No one should be denied this, and no one should be denied sharing their experiences in writing or punished for doing so. Thanks also to people on the outside who support their friends and family members who are trying to survive inside. We know that prison and jail take a toll on family and friends too. We know that family and friends of incarcerated people feel the surveillance and the scrutiny and the stereotypes that imprisoned people feel (Kotova, 2019). So we offer this issue to you in thanks for all the work that you do in trying to keep one another safe in this world, and for all of the solidarity that you share with one another. People expressing solidarity and mutual aid, you are the ones creating the circles of trust and belonging and care that are replacing the abuse, neglect, and harm of the criminal justice system.

REFERENCES

Ben-Moshe, Liat (2020) *Decarcerating Disability: Deinstitutionalization and Prison Abolition*, Minneapolis: University of Minnesota Press.

DiZoglio, Joseph David and Kate Telma (2022) "Proposing Abolition Theory for Carceral Medical Education", *Journal of Medical Humanities*, 43(2): 335-342.

Hancock, Philip and Yvonne Jewkes (2011) "Architectures of Incarceration: The Spatial Pains of Imprisonment", *Punishment & Society*, 13(5): 611-629.

Harkin, Diarmaid M. (2015) "The Police and Punishment: Understanding the Pains of Policing", *Theoretical Criminology*, 19(1): 43-58.

Kilgore, James and Brian Dolinar (2023) "Cages Without Bars Are Widening the Net: The Explosion of Electronic Monitoring", *Prison Legal News* – January 2023. Retrieved from: https://www.prisonlegalnews.org/news/2023/jan/1/cages-without-bars-are-widening-net-explosion-electronic-monitoring/

Kotova, Anna (2019) "'Time... lost time': Exploring How Partners of Long-term Prisoners Experience the Temporal Pains of Imprisonment", *Time & Society*, 28(2): 478-498.

Laniyonu, Ayobami (2022) "Phantom Pains: The Effect of Police Killings of Black Americans on Black British Attitudes", *British Journal of Political Science*, 52(4): 1651-1667.

Moran, Dominique (2012) "'Doing Time' in Carceral Space: Timespace and Carceral Geography", *Geografiska Annaler: Series B, Human Geography*, 94(4): 305-316.

Moran, Dominique, Jennifer Turner and Anne Schliehe (2018) "Conceptualizing the Carceral in Carceral Geography", *Progress in Human Geography*, 42(5): 666-686.

Paynter, Martha, Keisha Jefferies, Leah Carrier and Lorie Goshin (2022) "Feminist Abolitionist Nursing", *Ans. Advances in Nursing Science*, 45(1): 53-68.

Pollack, Shoshana and Christine Mayor (eds.) (2023) Special Issue – Walls to Bridges, *Journal of Prisoners on Prisons*, 32(1): 1-186.

Silverstein, Martin (2001) "The Ties that Bind: Family Surveillance of Canadian Parolees", *The Sociological Quarterly*, 42(3): 395-420.

Skinns, Layla and Andrew Wooff (2021) "Pain in Police Detention: A Critical Point in the 'Penal Painscape'?", *Policing and Society*, 31(3): 245-262.

Wang, Jackie (2018) *Carceral Capitalism*, Boston: MIT Press.

Weaver, Vesla M. and Amy E. Lerman (2010) "Political Consequences of the Carceral State", *American Political Science Review*, 104(4): 817-833.

ABOUT THE ISSUE EDITORS

Kevin Walby is an Associate Professor in the Department of Criminal Justice and Director of the Centre for Access to Information and Justice (CAIJ) at the University of Winnipeg. He is co-author of *Police Funding, Dark Money, and the Greedy Institution* (Routledge, 2022), as well as co-editor of *Disarm, Defund, Dismantle: Police Abolition in Canada* (BTL Press,

2022) and *Changing of the Guards: Private Influences, Privatization, and Criminal Justice in Canada* (UBC Press, 2022). He is also co-editor of the *Journal of Prisoners on Prisons*.

Justin Piché, PhD is Associate Professor in the Department of Criminology and Director of the Carceral Studies Research Collective at the University of Ottawa. He is also a member of the Criminalization and Punishment Education Project and Co-editor of the *Journal of Prisoners on Prisons*. During the COVID-19 pandemic, he has been tracking coronavirus infections and measures in Canadian jails, prisons, and penitentiaries as part of the Prison Pandemic Partnership.

ARTICLES

The Illusion of Parole
Gordon Pack

After serving 12 years and 11 months of a life sentence, I became eligible for parole consideration in 1992. However, 26 years and ten parole hearings later, I still do not know what I must do to obtain parole, and will they ever release me nor when or if I will ever be released. I am among a growing segment of men and women likely to die in prison because Maryland's parole scheme lacks discretionary standards and guidelines affording meaningful release consideration.

Maryland courts impose three distinct terms of life: (1) life with parole eligibility after serving 15 years less earned diminution credit; (2) life with parole eligibility after serving 25 years less earned diminution credit; and (3) life without the possibility of parole.[1] Prior to the birth of Maryland's notorious "life means life" standard, lifers were recommended and approved for release regularly. According to the Maryland Justice Policy, Inc., 92 of 155 lifers recommended for parole were released between 1970 and 1978; 65 of 88 lifers recommended for parole were released between 1979 and 1986; and 36 of 91 lifers recommended for parole were released between 1987 and 1994.[2] However, only one prisoner serving a life sentence has been paroled outright since 1994.

Parole is a conditional early release from a prison sentence.[3] For prisoners other than lifers, parole is viewed as an integral component of penal policy as it incentivizes good behaviour, serving as a reward for rehabilitation, a management tool to limit overcrowding, and to cut the costs of incarceration. Traditionally, Maryland Courts have held that the mere existence of a parole system does not create a constitutionally protected liberty interest.[4] As early release from a prison sentence is a privilege, prisoners do not have a constitutional right to be paroled. However, do parole eligible lifers have a legal right to meaningful parole consideration? In 1999, the MD Court of Special Appeals answered:

> Under the Maryland statutory scheme, until the Governor approves a parole recommendation for a lifer, and the court serves the inmate with an Order for Parole, the inmate has no due process right to parole or a parole hearing, and thus, has no liberty interest in meaningful parole consideration. Because appellant does not have a liberty interest in

meaningful parole consideration, the Governor's pronouncement does not offend any procedural due process concerns.[5]

Thus, no prisoner had a liberty interest in meaningful parole consideration in Maryland until a ruling in August 2018 by the Court of Appeals. Reviewing a trilogy of recent US Supreme Court opinions distinguishing juvenile from adult offenders, and mandating states to develop schemes for compliance, Maryland's highest court opined that a juvenile cannot be sentenced to life without a realistic and meaningful opportunity for release based on demonstrated maturity and rehabilitation.[6] As the vast majority of offenders are adults, 90 percent of Maryland's 2,300 lifer population is sadly not legally entitled to meaningful parole consideration. Without public interest, political advocacy, legislated standards, guidelines, and mandates to look beyond the original offenses of lifers, life sentences will continue to mean the rest of a prisoner's natural life behind bars regardless of their circumstances. The lack of standards and guidelines for the exercise of discretion in statutory and regulatory provision enables Maryland's dysfunctional system of parole. The failings of the parole scheme become apparent when examining the parole process in light of the Maryland Annotated Code Correctional Services Articles, the state's Code of Regulations (COMAR), and Division of Correction policy.

The Maryland Annotated Code is the official codification of statutory laws of the State, which is divided into 36 named articles. This Annotated Code is amended through the Maryland General Assembly, which is the legislative process where a 47-member elected Senate and a 141-member elected House of Delegates convene to introduce and vote on bills proposing change, repeal, or additions to existing state law. COMAR is the official compilation of all administrative regulations issued by state agencies governing the execution of duties authorized by the Annotated Code.

The Maryland Parole Commission (MPC) and general statutes governing the parole process were created by the General Assembly. Pursuant to this legislative authority, the MPC enacted regulations governing its policies. However, the legislature only authorized the MPC to recommend parole for prisoners serving sentences of life, while the Governor retains exclusive power to grant parole in such cases.[7]

The MPC consists of ten commissioners appointed by the Secretary of the Department of Public Safety and Correctional Services (DPSCS) and approved by the Governor and the Senate.[8] A two-commissioner panel is required to conduct a so-called parole hearing in the case of an eligible lifer. The in-person or video conference interview can hardly be described as an actual parole hearing because the panel lacks the authority to grant parole or even recommend it.

The interviewing panel is authorized to: 1) refuse parole, 2) schedule a future rehearing, or 3) refer a case for *en banc* proceedings where the full commission votes to make a recommendation to the Governor.[9] As there is no appeal from a decision by the two-commissioner panel, the interview is not electronically or stenographically recorded. The lack of a record makes judicial review of a decision impractical.

Attendance is restricted to parole personnel, an institutional case management representative, and the victim and/or victim representative(s). Upon request up to 30 days prior to the hearing, three advocates, whether legal representatives, relatives, or friends, may schedule a meeting on behalf of the prisoner. A single commissioner meets with the advocate(s) and not necessarily either one assigned to the hearing.[10]

In determining whether a prisoner is suitable for parole, Correctional Services Articles and COMAR require commissioners to consider and examine specific factors and information during the hearing.[11] Six youth related factors for juveniles were added to COMAR in 2016 in response to civil litigation over Maryland failing to provide them with meaningful parole consideration.[12]

Yet, statutes and regulations do not establish a standard for how these factors, criteria, information, and determinants should be assessed regarding parole consideration. After considering the identified factors, the MPC is free to accord more, less, or no weight to any of the factors. Whether factors should support or go against parole or should be considered aggravating or mitigating are not specified. Thus, the absence of any standards for the exercise of discretion enables decisions to be made on any basis.

For instance, the nature of the crime, the severity of the crime, and the person's prior criminal history are explicit factors to be considered. These factors can never change and often overshadow what has changed in a prisoner's life. Sentencing courts have considered these same factors when determining the length of a sentence imposed and when a criminalized person will become eligible for parole. Statutory law even permits sentencing judges to make recommendations to the MPC. Yet, the MPC is allowed to render judgment that a case warrants stiffer penalty.

My initial appearance before the MPC in 1999 illustrates the danger of discretionary autonomy and how parole hearings have been reduced to meaningless formalities. My five prior parole appearances were before Patuxent Institution's Board of Review (IBR). The IBR is an independent authority, which conducts annual progress reviews of prisoners in Patuxent's voluntary treatment programs. The IBR can grant, deny, as well as revoke eligibility and conditional release statuses. The IBR can also recommend early release from sentences after three years of participation in treatment programs.

Noting that I was seven years beyond my parole eligibility date, my last disciplinary infraction was in 1986, and my outstanding record of achievements, the MPC panel scheduled my case for a rehearing in 2009. According to one commissioner, the norm was to issue ten-year set-offs at a lifer's initial hearing. Adding insult to injury, another commented that I would have been better off having killed someone. I do not know what disturbed me the most – the implication that rape is a more egregious offense than murder deserving of greater punishment or that I would have to serve twice as much time than the law required to be considered for parole.

The lack of discretionary constraint is more alarming in the case of a refusal which every lifer dreads. As stated previously, one of the three options available to the panel is to refuse future parole consideration for any reason. Depriving future parole consideration to a prisoner sentenced to a parole eligible life term forecloses any possibility of release. Though perfectly legal according to statute, such decisions are contrary to legislative and judicial intent. Why should commissioners be permitted to effectively transform a sentence into life without parole without due process?

An anomaly surfaced in 1994, which the legislature has yet to redress. When parole eligibility was amended requiring people convicted of violent offences and sentenced to determinate terms to serve half of their sentences before qualifying for parole, parole eligibility for lifers remained the same. Parole Commissioners therefore cannot reasonably consider a lifer for parole upon eligibility in 15 or 25 years less earned diminution credit, when someone serving a lesser term of 50 years has to serve 25 years day for day before being considered for parole. Subsequently, lifers, even those sentenced in the 1960s, 1970s, and 1980s are expected to serve significantly longer periods behind bars before parole becomes even the slightest possibility.

Though not mandated by statute or regulation, Parole Commissioners now require a lifer to undergo a risk assessment before referral for *en banc* proceedings. While the use of risk assessment tools have become more prevalent nationwide, the MPC relies upon two openly biased indicators. The Violence Risk Appraisal guide (VRAG) and the Lifestyle Criminality Screening Form-Revised (LCSF-R) are static actuarial based risk assessment instruments. The individual's score is based on unchanging historical variables. No adjustments are made for a prisoner's current circumstances, the setting into which he will be released, their participation in treatment, education and vocational programming, nor developmental experiences occurring during incarceration.[13] Obviously, the static nature of these particular instruments is problematic for they do not take into account maturity and rehabilitation.

In addition, the nature of the convicted offense, multitude of convictions, and the age of the person at the time of the offenses elevate the assessment of recidivism and reduce the probability of being recommended for parole. These tests penalize criminalized people for committing crimes as children who have no adult experience in the outside community because they require greater supervision. There is even criticism regarding the applicability of these instruments in the cases of lifers. What pool of former prisoners can serve as the basis to predict recidivism for prisoners incarcerated for 30, 40, and 50 years? The attempt becomes more complex when considering the rare cases of lifers enduring long-term confinement for crimes committed as mid-teens. Research compiled on short-term prisoners is an inadequate barometer for the behaviour of lifers. Yet, those assessed to pose high risk of recidivism are not recommended to the Governor.

If the two-commissioner panel chooses to refer a lifer for the risk assessment, the parole decision is placed on hold pending the results. Unfortunately, the assessment is conducted by a lone MPC psychologist. The referral waiting list is 18 months long to this date. Typically, if a prisoner is assessed to be a moderate to low risk for recidivism, the case is referred for *en banc* proceedings.

As the risk assessments are conducted on behalf of the MPC and the Governor, the results are considered privileged and not provided to prisoners. I did not learn that I had been assessed at moderate to high risk for recidivism in 2012 until my 2015 rehearing. I was then told that I would not qualify for another risk assessment referral until five years had elapsed. Though grateful for the 2017 referral, I remain clueless about what I need to do to improve my assessment. In all actuality, seven years will have passed between opportunities for my case to possibly be considered for *en banc* proceedings.

Statutory law merely authorizes *en banc* proceedings before the MPC and that a majority vote is required before a recommendation is forwarded to the Governor. No criteria or factors have been established to guide the MPC's discretion during the proceedings. Neither do statutory and regulatory provisions specify what constitutes a quorum for voting purposes. Prisoners are not even notified of their cases being referred for these proceedings. More importantly, they do not have any input in this critical stage of the decision-making process. The MPC is shrouded in secrecy not bound by open records and disclosure laws.

Recommendations for the release of lifers have steadily decreased. Despite the MPC being authorized to make recommendations of parole to the Governor, rare recommendations for sentence commutation have become the norm. Statute does allow for the MPC to make recommendations for sentence commutation in the cases of lifers when warranted by special circumstances.[14] Apparently, all cases of lifers warrant such special consideration. A commutation to a determinate number of years allows for the gradual release of a former lifer. A recommendation for a delayed parole release would accomplish the same. The sad reality is that the MPC has rarely made parole recommendations for lifers over the past 20 odd years. No recommendations were made at all during some of those years.

Division of Correction policy has contributed to the shift in recommendations. In 1993, public outcry eschewed when a lifer in a work release program murdered his estranged girlfriend and committed suicide. The Commissioner of Corrections removed all prisoners serving life sentences from minimum security and pre-release facilities. The following year, a Division of Correction Directive (DCD) was promulgated excluding lifers from progressing below medium security institutions unless within three years of release.[15] This DCD has effectively barred lifers from participation in re-entry programming, which is only available in lower security facilities. Naturally, the MPC is reluctant to recommend the release of prisoners serving long-term confinement without a gauge of suitability for release.

Clearly, MPC recommendations are influenced by the reluctance of Governors to grant approval. Even the cases posing the lowest risk of recidivism could have huge political risks. Who can forget the derailment of former Massachusetts' Governor Dukakis' 1988 presidential campaign? The media sensationalized how Willie Horton, a prisoner Dukakis approved for work release, escaped, and raped a woman in Maryland. Commuting the sentence of a lifer to a determinate term of years therefore allows the MPC to assume the responsibility for the release and insulates the Governor.

In 1995, the politicization of the parole process for lifers became clear when former Governor Parris Glendening, suffering in the popularity polls, pronounced his "life means life" standard. He publicly rejected the parole recommendations of seven lifers, announced that he would not parole any lifer unless elderly or terminally ill, and also instructed the Parole Commission not to send any recommendations for lifers to his office.[16] Successive governors followed the same standard not wanting to appear soft on violent crime. Two decades later, former Governor Glendening would admit his standard created a dysfunctional system.[17]

Nonetheless, Maryland's parole scheme has always been subject to dysfunction. The lack of standards and guidelines enables the discriminatory practice which has lasted for over two decades. Maryland is one of three states which require gubernatorial approval for prisoners serving life to be paroled. Unlike Oklahoma and California, Maryland statutory law establishes no criteria for the Governor's exercise of parole discretion. Until 2011, the Governor was free to approve, disapprove, or ignore recommendations by the Parole Commission without providing any justification.

In the wake of recommendations stagnating in the Governor's Office for years, legislators amended the statute to allow the recommendation of the Parole Commission to take effect if the Governor does not disapprove it within 180 days. The reaction of sitting Governor Martin O'Malley was to disapprove recommendations in 57 cases before the deadline.[18] This amendment applies to recommendations for parole, not recommendations for commutation. Though the legislature established a timeframe for the Governor's decision, he may continue to deny parole for any reason, without any standards, explanation, or opportunity for review.

Following in the wake of Supreme Court's decision to prohibit the imposition of a life without parole sentence on a juvenile, because the sentence does not provide an opportunity for meaningful parole consideration based on demonstrated maturity and rehabilitation, I was one of the juvenile lifers who challenged the legality of parole eligible life sentences in Maryland.[19] The argument was simply that Maryland's parole scheme operates as a system of *ad hoc* executive clemency, which does not comply with the Supreme Court's mandate for states to develop mechanisms for compliance. To my dismay, a 3/4 majority the Court of Appeals ruled that Maryland's life sentences imposed on juveniles were made legal by the 2016 amended regulations, requiring consideration of six youth related factors by the MPC, and a controversial Executive Order issued by Governor Paul Hogan in 2018, binding himself and successive Governors to consider the same factors as the MPC.[20]

Mere consideration of youth related factors cannot bring Maryland's dysfunctional system into compliance. The parole scheme operates as a system of executive clemency in which opportunities for release are extremely rare, unpredictable, and shrouded in secrecy. Virtually no one is ever paroled. The remote possibility of release is insufficient. Thus, consideration is not enough! Without standards guiding the exercise of discretion by the decision makers, the possibility of parole is an empty promise. Any system that does not allow for a juvenile sentenced to life to be released upon demonstration of maturity and rehabilitation violates the Eighth Amendment. If the Maryland sentence is cruel and unusual punishment for children, how can the identical sentence be fair for adults? The possibility of parole must be more than an illusion.

Advocates have been trying to persuade the General Assembly to remove the gubernatorial requirement since 1998 to no avail. If the legislature insists that the Governor should have the final say in the release of lifers, it must enact criteria, standards, and guidelines for the exercise of discretion, and an avenue for review. Did the Governor have the authority to bind himself and future governors with the 2018 Executive Order or does the authority to fetter the Governor's discretion rest squarely upon the shoulders of the General Assembly? More importantly, when considering the Executive Order can be rescinded at anytime, cannot be enforced, does not apply to recommendations of commutation, does not instruct the MPC to resume making recommendations for parole, and provides no standards for gubernatorial discretion, one wonders if the objective was simply to usurp the judgment of the Court. The Order was issued three days after oral arguments on the legality of life sentences imposed upon juvenile offenders appeared to go against the state.

While reform efforts have focused on the Governor's role in the parole process, attention should be directed to the statutory and regulatory provisions related to the MPC. The legislature and the judiciary should insist that the MPC resumes making recommendations for parole, rather than for commutation in the case of lifers as authorized by statute. Commutation of sentence is a standard-less act of clemency by which the Governor substitutes a lesser penalty than imposed by the Court.[21] It does not enable prisoners to predict when they may be released. This rarity should not be the normal expectation because statutory and regulatory provisions specify when one becomes eligible for parole, as well as detail a procedure and standards for parole.

The promulgation of standards and guidelines for the exercise of parole discretion by the MPC and the Governor are critical to providing meaningful release opportunities. Provisions could instruct how to assess rehabilitation, how to give weight to certain factors, how to gauge risk assessment instruments, and other quantitative guides, to require rendering specific findings of fact to support decisions, as well as provide prisoners with specific objectives to obtain a MPC recommendation and parole.

Lifers should be recommended for parole upon or shortly after reaching eligibility as intended by the legislature and judiciary. As the sentencing judges are aware of parole eligibility affixed to particular sentences, prisoners are expected to be paroled as specified unless noted otherwise. The severity of the underlying offense was also considered before the imposition of a sentence.

The presumption of rehabilitation should be the norm unless a delay is warranted by a prisoner's misbehaviour or an unambiguous threat posed to public safety. The anomaly that exists in parole eligibility for determinate and indeterminate sentences needs to be redressed. If public sentiment is for lifers to serve longer terms of confinement, then the parole eligibility requirement must be raised from 15 and 25 years less earned diminution credit. This amendment should not be applied retroactively.

A mandatory release date could be enacted for the two parole eligible life terms. For instance, a sentence could require a minimum of 15 years and a maximum of 25 years or a minimum of 25 years and a maximum of 40 years subject to life for parole violation. Would a mandatory release date of 60 years applicable to diminution credit really depreciate the weight of a criminal offense?

The Commissioner of Correction's rationale for restricting lifers to medium and above security facilities is that prisoners with no hope for release pose a significant threat to public safety. It is shameful that every lifer is being penalized for actions of one lifer 25 years ago. Hope could be restored by the MPC recommending delayed parole releases and the Governor approving these releases. The re-entry programming available in lesser security facilities is critical for those who serve long-term incarceration.

In response to civil litigation in the Federal District by the ACLU for Maryland juvenile lifers, a Division of Correction Directive was promulgated allowing the security level of juvenile lifers to be decreased if approved by the Commissioner.[22] Thus far, the only juvenile lifers transferred to minimum security facilities were two of the three principle complainants represented in the lawsuit who happen to have recommendations for commutation pending in the Governor's Office.

At the very least, statutory and regulatory provisions should distinguish juveniles from adults. Juveniles are less culpable and more likely to change than adults. The juvenile is also subject to spend a disproportionate number of years behind bars than the adult simply because of their youth. While legislatures in states across the country have taken significant measures to amend parole statutes and regulations to comply with the Supreme Court mandate for juveniles, the Maryland legislature has done nothing.

Perhaps, this is a reflection of public sentiment. No one cares whether the parole system is just. Society is fed up with violent crime and lifers are the scapegoats. Most believe that life should mean life and those who commit capital offenses cannot be rehabilitated. However, ignoring the law and mistreating others is a crime, even when it relates to criminals.

The ending of the Court of Appeals' Chief Judge Mary Ellen Barbera's dissenting opinion in the recent juvenile lifer cases is befitting:

And it is not justice to have on the books the "possibility of parole" yet provide a protocol for granting or denying parole that is without standards to guide those who are the decision makers: the Parole Commission and the Governor. Under the United States Constitution, a meaningful opportunity for release cannot exist in name only, as it now does in Maryland.[23]

Since the initial August 2019 submission of this article for publication, there have been two relevant changes to Maryland's parole scheme. Firstly, the static risk assessment instruments relied upon by the MPC and the

Governor were replaced by another instrument in August of 2020. This new tool is reportedly dynamic in nature, which allows the clinical psychologists who administer the assessment to include post-crime factors rendering lower risk ratings.

Secondly, in December 2021, the General Assembly, with a two-thirds majority vote in the Senate and the House of Delegates, overrode Governor Hogan's veto of a bill removing the gubernatorial requirement for a release lifer on parole. Although this amendment significantly reduces the politicization of MD's parole process related to lifers, the General Assembly has yet to create any standards for the MPC's exercise of discretion. The MPC thus remains free to deny or grant the release of prisoners for any reason and without explanation.

ENDNOTES

[1]   MD Code Ann., Criminal Law Article§ 2 and MD Code Ann., Corr. Servs. Article § 7.
[2]   *Lifers Paroles in Maryland* (1970- 2008) by Frank Dunbaugh, J.D., Maryland Justice Policy, Inc., 2008.
[3]   MD Code Ann., Corr. Servs. Article§ 7-lOl(c).
[4]   Mclaughlin-Cox v. MD Parole Commission, 200 Md. App. 115 (2011).
[5]   Lomax v. Warden, 120 Md. App. 314, 329-30 (1999).
[6]   Carter v. State, MD Court of Appeals, No. 54, September Term, 2017 and Bowie v. State, MD Court of Appeals, No. 55, September Term, 2017.
[7]   COMAR 12.08.0l.17.A(7)(e).
[8]   MD Code Ann., Corr. Servs. Article§ 7-202.
[9]   COMAR 12.08.01.17.A (7)(f) and (g).
[10]   COMAR 12.08.0l.18©(l).
[11]   MD Code Ann., Corr. Servs. Article§ 7-305 and COMAR 12.08.01.17.
[12]   COMAR 12.08 .01.17 (2016).
[13]   Brief of Amici Curiae by the University of Baltimore Juvenile Justice Project in Bowie v. State, MD Court of Appeals, September Term (2017).
[14]   COMAR 12.08.01.15 (B).
[15]   DCD 100.5.
[16]   "Glendening to reject parole in life sentences" by Charles Babington, *The Washington Post*, September 22, 1995.
[17]   "Md. Lawsuit over juvenile lifers part of nationwide trend" by Juliet Linderman, *The Daily Record*, August 3, 2017.
[18]   "Assembly seat highlights O' Malley's views on crime" by Aaron Davis, *The Washington Post*, December 2, 2012.
[19]   Graham v. Florida, 560 US 48 (2010); Miller v. Alabama, 132, S.Ct. 2455 (2012); and Montgomery v. Louisiana, 136 S.Ct. 718 (2016).
[20]   James Bowie v. State of Maryland, Court of Appeals, # 55, September Term, 2017.

[21] MD Code Ann., Corr. Servs. Article§ 7-101 (d).
[22] Executive Directive Number OPS.100.4.
[23] Concurring and Dissenting Opinion in Bowie v. State, Court of Appeals, No# 55, September Term, 2017.

ABOUT THE AUTHOR

Gordon Pack is serving an aggregate sentence of life with the possibility of parole for rape, kidnapping, and armed robbery offenses committed as a 15-year-old. A 2020 parole decision in Gordon's case remains on hold pending another risk assessment and possible *en banc* proceedings. He has been incarcerated in the Maryland Division of Correction since 1980. Though his first five years of imprisonment were plagued with adjustment issues, he managed to turn his life around, becoming a model prisoner. He engages in various cognitive behaviour therapy, conflict resolution, alternatives to violence, juvenile counselling, and community service programs. He is a long-standing member of the Lifers' Groups advocating for prison reform, rehabilitative and reentry services, victim awareness, and peer mentoring. He credits his reformation to remedial programs at Patuxent Institution, conversion to Orthodox Islam, and the loyal support of family, friends, and advocates. He can be contacted at:

Gordon Pack
MCI-J, SID# 250505
P.O. Box 549
Jessup, MD 20794, USA

ANTWERP'S BEGIJNENSTRAAT
THEN AND NOW

Almost half a century ago, in 1973, I was locked up for a month in the prison of the Begijnenstraat in Antwerp. I was 20 years old when I got to know for the first time about the interior of a police station, then a cell in the basement of the Antwerp courthouse, followed by a prison cell, the one in Begijnenstraat,[1] and finally with a courtroom.

As a young activist, I had joined about 20 other people from Alle Macht aan de Arbeiders (AMADA, All Power to the Workers), a Maoist organization, in the dockers' strike of April-May-June 1973 in Antwerp and Ghent, a so-called wildcat strike – that is to say, a strike not recognized by the trade unions. It was the period "after May 68". AMADA was looking for a candidate to be its spokesperson in this strike and that is how I became the man with the megaphone. This would lead to my arrest and imprisonment, after a violent clash between police, strikers and activists on May 14, 1973.[2]

The incident took place during a demonstration in which women dockworkers were beaten by the police armed with truncheons, to prevent them from going to the building of the ABVV (Flemish FGTB) union offices to claim strike pay. Some of the demonstrators, noticing that a police car from the specialist surveillance unit – the Brigade de Surveillance et de Recherche (BSR) (Surveillance & Research Brigade) – was tailing the demonstration, broke off. The violence they had just seen inflicted by truncheon-wielding officers on the mothers and sisters of the strikers had provoked anger and a culprit was needed. A few hours later, after the gendarmerie hermetically sealed the dockers' recruitment office, the public prosecutor issued an arrest warrant in my name. But a dock worker had hidden me under a blanket in the back seat of his car and I was able to escape, although not for long. On May 15, I was sent to prison. One month later, on the day the strike ended, I was released.

MEMORIES OF THE BEGIJNENSTRAAT

Short as my prison stay was – many of my comrades received far heavier sentences in the years to come – I have vivid memories of my few weeks

28

stay in the Begijnenstraat. And it is probably one of the reasons why I became a prison teacher a couple of decades later.

I remember entering the prison and being stripped of every personal belonging. I received oversized shoes and an oversized uniform – they did not have my size, they said. I remember my little cell. Eating there alone with the plastic toilet bucket next to the table. The lack of daylight. The once a week shower. Walking in the yard every day for an hour. Limited contact with other prisoners and the sensation of the ways in which aggression, poverty, and social misery were concentrated in the prison. Military-style orders from some guards if you shout something out of your cell window to your fellow walkers. The light that turns on and off at a fixed time. No television, but a radio, the volume of which could not be adjusted. Then, there was the older prisoner, crying like a child in the prison car that transported us to the courthouse. A contraband cigarette and matches were in the cell in the basement of the Antwerp Court house, as we waited to go to the council chambers. My mother and my sister visiting me and the way my mother cried when she saw me behind glass and in prison clothes.

It was my introduction to a world that cannot produce anything positive, if only because concentrating people 'in difficulty' in one place can only create more difficulties. But at the time, the prison was anything but overcrowded. I saw no rats or other vermin there. No mattresses on the floor. Having an individual cell was not a problem at the time. And surely one could only expect that over time things would get better and more humane?

FROM OVERCROWDING
TO THE 'PRISON VILLAGE'

In 1995, Stefaan De Clerck became Minister of Justice in the Dehaene government.[3] On June 12 1996, he wrote the "Orientation Note on Criminal Policy and Penitentiary Policy", which came to be considered by "academics, lawyers and politicians as the new starting point for Belgian penal and penitentiary policy".[4] In this policy document, the minister both pleads for fewer prisons and opposes the harmful effects of the long-term deprivation of liberty. With a more selective use of the prison sentence, the locking up of fewer people as a preventive measure and shorter sentences, the current situation could change, says the minister. More work needs to be done on provisional release based on an individual assessment of the prisoner. Priority must be given to measures aimed at rehabilitation and reintegration.

What happened to this policy document? It quickly disappeared into the wastebasket.[5] I doubt even the current Minister of Justice, Van Quickenborne, has ever seen or read this text from 1996. I doubt if he knows about the existence of the texts of 2008, also promising the humanization of prisons (i.e. "The Master Plan Detention and Internment Under Humane Conditions")[6] of another Minister of Justice, Jo Vandeurzen, the successor of De Clerck.

Be that as it may, what is the current situation now in 2022, 25 years after De Clerck's intervention? In an opinion published in *De* Standaard,[7] Van Quickenborne[8] outlines his "new ideas on prisons". Van Quickenborne announces a revolution, certainly an incremental one, but a revolution all the same. The minister declared no clear choices were made in the past and too little was invested. We now know the consequences. High rates of recidivism, inflated sentences and overcrowding that has gone on for decades, he notes. But today, according to his plan, everything will change. "Beneath the waterline, a silent revolution is taking place in the prison system". So exactly what is the nature of this "silent revolution'" and how does Van Quickenborne intend to capitalize on it? By investing millions of Euros, creating the new post of detention guides (aside the prison guards) to monitor detainee's individual detention plan, and by building new prisons in Brussels-Haren and Dendermonde. According to the Minister, the prison at Haren will become the model prison of the future: "A prison village: a sum of small entities in which we live as a community". Seven halfway houses, adding up to 450 new places, and 15 additional detention houses will also be created, thus creating 720 more places, and it is claimed that detention will be individualized. That is, from now on, detainees will leave prison in a better position than when they entered it.

At the same time, the minister wants to increase the number of prisoners. Yes, from the first of June all shorter prison sentences will be executed (until now the sentences of less than three years were often not executed). From that date on, some 700 extra persons are expected to enter the already overcrowded prisons. But, announces the minister, those short sentences will take place in detention facilities for between 20 to 60 people. By effectively executing the shorter sentences, magistrates will be freed from the burden of imposing increasingly severe sentences because of recidivism.

REPLICATING THE LOGIC OF
THE OLD PRISON SYSTEM

Far from being new, Van Quickenborne's so-called new ideas remind me of the beginning of the modern prison 200 years ago. Then, too, the grand narrative was about making punishment more humane, while the underlying reality was less savory: the evolution of new punishments and other forms of violence, such as solitary confinement and permanent observation. Van Quickenborne has absolutely no intention of reducing the number of prisoners and even less of questioning the prison institution. Like his predecessors, the minister deals with the consequences of crime and never what creates it, what precedes prison – a social model of profit and inequality, a lack of care, education, housing and work. Under Van Quickenborne there will be more detention, but it will be in "a penal village like Haren where people live together as a community"[9] or in detention houses. All this is constructed on the neoliberal model of individualization of guilt and punishment, a model that refuses to seek responsibilities and solutions at the collective and societal level.

THE COUNTER-REVOLUTION
IN PRACTICE

Since the 1980s, the situation in Belgian prisons has only got worse. Every decade, politicians promise to reform the penitentiary system is repeated. So why is the situation for prisoners worse today than it was half a century ago?

If there has been a turning point, it is in the opposite direction to progress. Like most other European countries, Belgium's punitive shift from the 1980s involved adopting a harsher detention policy and longer sentences. Between 1980 and 2000, the number of detainees in Belgium rose from 5,000 to more than 11,000, which contributed to a situation where prisons became out of control. The case of the Antwerp prison illustrates this.

On May 6, 1999, the headline in the Flemish newspaper *De Standaard* was "Severe overcrowding in Antwerp prison". On that date, there were 450 detainees for 285 places (an occupancy rate of 157 percent), compared to 760 detainees for 440 places today (an occupancy rate of 172 percent).

In 2003, Antwerp's Begijnenstraat was already the subject of a fairly lively debate within the Committee for Welfare, Public Health and Equal Opportunities that centered on overcrowding and an "explosive situation" aggravated by "degrading conditions". By 2003, prison guards at the Begijnenstraat had acted against this state of affairs over four years! In February 2003, they went on a work-to-rule strike that involved blocking access to prison for 60 social workers for 11 weeks, which resulted in two months of technical unemployment for them.[10]

Two years later, in 2005, nothing was resolved and the newspapers, including those abroad, spoke of the "medieval conditions in the prison of Antwerp".[11] Ten years later, in 2015, and nothing had changed. Nagib Amari found himself in this same prison for three months after the discovery of a cannabis plantation in a warehouse he rented. An unfair accusation, as it turned out later when Nagib was fully acquitted. But during the three months of his detention, he contracted a serious eye infection that was so badly treated that he almost completely lost the use of his left eye. In prison, he had to sleep on a mattress on the floor. There was an open toilet in the cell and he was only allowed to take a shower once a week due to the lack of staff. Nagib suffered from a serious eye disease and wore contact lenses. When he arrived in prison, he had to hand over the suction cups that he used to put on the contact lenses. He got them back three days later, but in the meantime, he had to remove his lenses with his hands. He had red eyes from his first day in prison, but he was not allowed to see an eye doctor at the hospital and had to settle for a prison doctor. When his wife came to bring him extra lens fluid, they refused to give it to him and he was told he had to buy the fluid through the prison. However, this was not possible, as his bank accounts had been blocked. After his release, Amari had to undergo 13 operations and filed a lawsuit against the Belgian state for the errors and the lack of medical care. The court ruled that he was entitled to compensation of 51,000 euros.[12] Small consolation for the loss of an eye and costs that amount to tens of thousands of euros.

In 2018, a Dutch newspaper wrote, "Suffering in the Antwerp cells: no ventilation, hot cells, no visitors and rats in the corridor. Conditions in the former prison in Antwerp are inhumane, Dutch inmates say".[13] Two years later, in November 2020, the Minister of Justice and the Mayor of Antwerp visited the prison. The mayor of Antwerp, Bart De Wever, repeated what was said 20 years earlier: "The situation is difficult, I'm going to have trouble falling asleep". He asked the Minister of Justice Vincent Van Quickenborne to quickly find a solution to the overcrowding.[14] Again, nothing changed. Perhaps a visit of GAIA (Global Action in the Interest of Animals) could help. They could certify that locking people up in cages has the same effect on humans as on chickens, rabbits, and other animals. All you have to do is replace the word 'animal' with the word 'human' in this statement from the animal rights organization: "Science shows that locking animals in cages is cruel. Animals have feelings and are capable of feeling pain and joy. Caging causes severe suffering because the animals are severely restricted in their movements and have few opportunities to express their natural behaviour. This leads to stress and frustration".[15]

2021: "MICE ON THE WALLS, MATTRESSES ON THE FLOOR"

In November 2021, Frederik Janssens wrote an opinion piece on behalf of the Antwerp Prison Supervisory Board, entitled: "Mice on the walls, mattresses on the floor".[16] In the piece, he gives the example of a prisoner locked up in the Begijnenstraat since April 2020. The man was sentenced to eight years in prison in August 2021. He wants to go to another prison and is on the transfer list to Leuven-Centraal but the management of the Begijnenstraat cannot decide on this independently. Meanwhile, the man finds himself with four people in a cell that is far too small. He sees the mice running on the walls. If the guards go on strike, it means no walks or showers. The prison can hold 439 prisoners, but as of mid-November, 769 people are locked up there. An occupancy rate of 175 percent. There is a big humidity problem, mould stains in several places and there is a smell of sewage. Prisoners can only take a shower on certain days – and then only if the water pressure is sufficient. On other days, they can ask for hot water to wash at their sink. Some complain of insect bites. In several cells, the pipes are broken, and it stinks. Attempts have been made to fix them with tape, but the tape is coming off. In other cells, peeling paint falls to the floor. The connection of the drainpipes to the ceiling is covered with newspaper. In some cells, the toilets are open and exposed next to the cell door, with no screen in front of them. The safety and health of staff and prisoners are thus endangered. Captives are crammed into cells that are tiny. Several imprisoned people do not have a bed. They sleep on a mattress on the floor. The stress in the cells increases, leading to more quarrels and violence. Staff can no longer guarantee the services to which prisoners are entitled. There are waiting lists for the fitness facilities and the library. Various activities are regularly cancelled due to lack of staff. Sports activities are limited. The health system is failing. The high demand for medical consultations has given rise to the famous one-minute consultations and it is necessary to wait several weeks for dentists. There is also a waiting list to be allowed to work as a prisoner.

The damning picture painted by Frederik Janssens, on behalf of the Antwerp Prison Surveillance Committee was followed by articles in the newspapers with some testimonies of prisoners and guards in the Begijnenstraat. "During the day we put that (third) mattress (in a 8m² cell) right against the wall, but even then, there is barely room to stretch our legs". Sitting at the table to eat is impossible, so the men do it on their beds or take turns. Food scraps and waste are everywhere in the cell, including the sink. It is not an uplifting environment. "We can do nothing but sit still on our bed and watch TV". A prison guard added:

> The prisoners say they have no breathing room. They become angry because activities to which they used to be entitled – sports, receiving visitors – are much less possible. Due to the size of the prison sections, we can only organize the walk once a day, because going outside with 200 is of no use to anyone. Then it's from one sardine can to the next. Taking a shower every day is no longer an option. Today it's the turn of the left side of the corridor, tomorrow the right side.

ARE THERE SOLUTIONS?

Solutions exist. A first solution consists in the immediate reduction of the number of prisoners incarcerated in the Begijnenstraat, by half. The second solution consists in the pure and simple closing of the prison, not in five years, but on the spot. If they think that these solutions are not possible, our political decision-makers have only to draw inspiration from the following two examples from the United States, their closest friend and ally.

In June 2011, a court ordered the state of California to end overcrowding in its 33 state prisons. Ten thousand prisoners, nearly 8 percent of all state detainees, were to be released by the end of the year, the court ruled. The judgment stated: "The overpopulation which has caused extreme suffering and even death must be ended. Depriving prisoners of their rights violates the Constitution, which prohibits cruel and inhuman treatment. This measure should improve medical and mental care in prisons". The state of California appealed but the Supreme Court upheld the judgment and ordered the state to reduce the number of prisoners by 33,000 over the next two years. After this court ruling, the state and prison administrations sought not to release prisoners but to transfer them from state prisons to local prisons. However, this in no way diminishes the importance of this historic verdict.[17]

There is another, more recent example. On August 26 2021, the Metropolitan Correctional Center (MCC), a prison in New York, was closed indefinitely due to "inhumane prison conditions". Two years earlier, Jeffrey Epstein had committed suicide there and in May 2020, an inspection revealed that "inmates showing symptoms of coronavirus were neglected and ignored". They found that there was virtually no physical distance between the prisoners and that "some of them slept on bunk beds within easy reach of each other".[18]

SPOT THE DIFFERENCES BETWEEN MCC AND BEGIJNENSTRAAT

In the Begijnenstraat, the prisoners no longer even sleep in bunk beds, but 62 of them sleep on a mattress on the floor. Deaths by suicide have also taken place there. In 2015, Nick Van Laethem hanged himself in the prison laundry room. Most recently, on October 26 2021, another prisoner committed suicide in his cell. The only real difference between the MCC and the Begijnenstraat is that one is closed and the other remains open.

The question arises as to whether anyone responsible for the current situation in the Antwerp prison will be prosecuted for failing to provide aid to persons in need, in this case the prisoners. Following the Belgian law:

> If help is not provided to a person in need, one risks a prison sentence of eight days to one year and a fine of € 400.00 up to and including € 4,000. The maximum prison sentence is increased to two years if the person in danger is a minor or is in a vulnerable condition due to age, pregnancy or illness or physical or mental infirmity or disability, if this condition was clearly known to the person who gave no help.[19]

If convicted upon the basis of this law, Belgian officials will for sure regret the day they decided to execute all prison sentences.

ENDNOTES

[1] The prison of Antwerp was built in 1854-59. Its architecture followed the example of the Pennsylvanian prison system and the concept of the English model prison of Pentonville, built in 1840-1842, with a regime of total cellular seclusion and a new type of prison architecture, namely the cell prison based on the panopticon plan. Several prisons in the country, including Tongeren, Brussels, Marche, Verviers, Liège, Charleroi, Dinant, Kortrijk, Bruges, and Leuven, were built following the same model. In 2020, Belgium counted 35 prisons. The official capacity of the prison system was 9,545 (as of 1 January 2021). The total prison population (including pre-trial detainees / remand prisoners) was 10,379 as of 31 January 2021 according to the Council of Europe. Source: https://www.prisonstudies.org/country/belgium

[2] A police colonel called Van Geet wrote the only book that exists on this strike entitled *De Dokstaking 1973* (The Dockstrike, 1973).

[3] Stefaan De Clerk (Christian Democratic and Flemish party) was Minister of Justice of Belgium from 1995 until 1998 and from 2008 until 2011.

[4] Source: https://libstore.ugent.be/fulltxt/RUG01/001/787/137/RUG01-001787 137_2012_0001_AC.pdf

[5] In 1996, in his note on penal policy, De Clerck clearly opposed the increase in prison capacity and advocated for the development of alternative penalties and measures. He made a U-turn 12 years later. In his complement to "The Masterplan Detention and Internment Under Humane Conditions", under the heading "Social Impact of Prisons", he promoted the construction of new prisons, highlighting the importance of the economic benefits of prisons, in terms of direct jobs (e.g. a prison with 444 places would provide 500 jobs for "at least 100 years") or indirect (local police for prisoner transport, prisoner aid organizations, houses of justice, various prison suppliers, etc.), not to mention the activity generated by the arrival of staff members settling in the region with their families (housing, shops, schools, etc.). Source: https://revueobservatoire.be/Place-sens-de-la-prison-en-Belgique-entre-discours-et-pratiques (extract from « La politique pénitentiaire », Philippe Mary, CRISP | 2012/12 n° 2137 | pages 5 to 47)

[6] The document entitled "The Masterplan for Detention and Internment in Humane Conditions" appeared in 2008. It outlined the long-term policy for detention in Belgium, centred around the construction of new prisons to humanize living conditions in prison. In the following years it was updated several times. The most recent edition dates from 2016. See: Masterplan 2008-2012-2016 pour une « infrastructure pénitentiaire dans des conditions humaines ». Sources: https://justice.belgium.be/ fr/nouvelles/communiques_de_presse/masterplan_2008_2012_2016_pour_une_ infrastructure_penitentiaire and https://news.belgium.be/fr/masterplan-prisons-iii-adaptation-du-masterplan-pour-une-detention-dans-des-conditions-humaines

[7] "De stille revolutie in onze gevangenissen" (The silent revolution in our prisons), *De Standaard*, by the Minister of Justice, Vincent Van Quickenborne – 1 May 2022.

[8] Since 2020, Vincent Van Quickenborne (Open Flemish Liberals and Democrats) is the actual Minister of Justice. He is the eightieth minister of Justice of Belgium during a period spanning twenty years.

9   See the critical report of the Central Prison Supervisory Board on Haren prison
    after their visit at the site under construction on 3 November 2021. Source: https://
    ccsp.belgium.be/wp-content/uploads/2021/12/Avis_Advies-Haren-Visite_Bezoek-
    nov.21FR.pdf
10 Meeting of the Committee for Welfare, Public Health and Equal Opportunities from
    the Flemish parliament on 6 May 2003. Source: https://docs.vlaamsparlement.be/
    website/htm-vrg/341633.html
11 The Dutch paper *Nederlands Dagblad* on the medieval conditions in Antwerp
    prison: https://www.nd.nl/nieuws/buitenland/687720/middeleeuwse-toestanden-in-
    antwerpse-gevangenis
12 "Man goes blind in one eye after wrongly staying in prison": https://www.pzc.nl/
    antwerpen/zakenman-raakt-blind-aan-een-oog-na-onterecht-verblijf-in-gevangenis-
    sinds-vrijlating-al-128-keer-op-consultatie-geweest~a8b3630b/?referrer=https-
    %3A%2F%2Fwww.google.com%2F
13 The Dutch paper *Algemeen Dagblad* article on the situation of Dutch detainees
    in Antwerp prison entitled "Suffocating in an Antwerp cell": https://www.ad.nl/
    buitenland/afzien-in-de-antwerpse-cel-niet-luchten-geen-bezoek-en-ratten-in-de-ga
    ng~afc52ea8/?referrer=https%3A%2F%2Fwww.google.com%2F
14 Bart De Wever on Facebook. Source: Thttps://www.facebook.com/bartdewever/
    photos/vandaag-bezocht-ik-de-gevangenis-in-de-begijnenstraat-om-er-te-praten-
    met-direct/10157627770327057/
15 Source: https://www.gaia.be/sites/default/files/campaigns/attachments/2018_-_
    stop_de_kooien_-_report_online_compressed.pdf
16 Source: https://www.standaard.be/cnt/dmf20211129_97638409
17 Source: https://www.npr.org/2011/05/23/136579580/california-is-ordered-to-cut-
    its-prison-population?t=1641485944852
18 Source: https://www.npr.org/2021/08/26/1031541974/u-s-closing-jail-jeffrey-
    epstein-metropolitan-correctional-center
19 "Guilty neglect: when should a person in need be helped?": https://www.
    destrafrechtspecialist.be

REFERENCES

Associated Press (2021) "U.S. is closing the troubled NYC jail where Jeffrey
    Epstein killed himself", *NPR News* – August. Retrieved from: https://www.
    npr.org/2021/08/26/1031541974/u-s-closing-jail-jeffrey-epstein-metropolitan-
    correctional-center
Belgian Federal Public Service, Justice (2008) "Masterplan 2008-2012-2016 pour
    une infrastructure pénitentiaire dans des conditions humaines". Retrieved from:
    https://justice.belgium.be/fr/nouvelles/communiques_de_presse/masterplan_2008_
    2012_2016_pour_une_infrastructure_penitentiaire
Centrale Toezichtsraad voor het Gevangeniswezen – Conseil Central de Surveillance
    Pénitentiaire (2021) "Avis du CCSP suite à la visite du site en construction de la
    prison de Haren (23.11.21)". Retrieved from: https://ccsp.belgium.be/wp-content/
    uploads/2021/12/Avis_Advies-Haren-Visite_Bezoek-nov.21FR.pdf

Commissie voor Welzijn, Volksgezondheid en Gelijke Kansen Vergadering van 06/05/2003. (2003) "Interpellatie van mevrouw Trees Merckx-Van Goey tot mevrouw Mieke Vogels, Vlaams minister van Welzijn, Gezondheid, Gelijke Kansen en Ontwikkelingssamenwerking, over de externe hulpverlening in de Antwerpse gevangenis". Retrieved from: https://docs.vlaamsparlement.be/website/htm-vrg/341633.html

Conseil des ministres du 18 novembre 2016 (2016) "Masterplan prisons III - Adaptation du masterplan pour une détention dans des conditions humaines"., Retrieved from: https://news.belgium.be/fr/masterplan-prisons-iii-adaptation-du-masterplan-pour-une-detention-dans-des-conditions-humaines

de Wever, Bart (2020) Facebook post. Retrieved from: https://www.facebook.com/bartdewever/photos/vandaag-bezocht-ik-de-gevangenis-in-de-begijnenstraat-om-er-te-praten-met-direct/10157627770327057/

Gaia (2021) "Stop de kooien 1,5 miljoen Europeanen tekenden de petitie!" Retrieved from: https://www.gaia.be/nl/campagnes/stop-de-kooien

Janssens, Frederik (2021) "Muizen op de muren, matrassen op de grond", *De Standard*. Retrieved from: https://www.standaard.be/cnt/dmf20211129_97638409

Mary, Philippe (2010) "Place et sens de la prison en Belgique: entre discours et pratiques", *L'Observatoire*, 66: 32-37.

Ouvry, Quinten (2010) "HET GEVANGENISBELEID ONDER MINISTER DE CLERCK Van reductionisme naar expansie Masterproef van de opleiding 'Master in de rechten'", Faculteit Rechtsgeleerdheid Universiteit Gent.

Thewissen, Pascale (2005) "Middeleeuwse toestanden in Antwerpse gevangenis. nederlands dagblad". Retrieved from: https://www.nd.nl/nieuws/buitenland/687720/middeleeuwse-toestanden-in-antwerpse-gevangenis

Totenberg, Nina (2011) "High Court Rules Calif. Must Cut Prison Population", *NPR* – May. Retrieved from: https://www.npr.org/2011/05/23/136579580/california-is-ordered-to-cut-its-prison-population?t=1641485944852

Van de Pol, Caroline (2020) "Zakenman raakt blind aan één oog na onterecht verblijf in gevangenis: 'Sinds vrijlating al 128 keer op consultatie geweest'", *PZC*. Retrieved from: https://www.pzc.nl/antwerpen/zakenman-raakt-blind-aan-een-oog-na-onterecht-verblijf-in-gevangenis-sinds-vrijlating-al-128-keer-op-consultatie-geweest~a8b3630b/?referrer=https%3A%2F%2Fwww.google.com%2F

Van Geen, Willy (1979) *De dokstaking 1973 : dagboek van een sociaal konflikt in de haven van Antwerpen en Gent*, Antwerpen, De Vlijt: Willy Publisher.

Voskuil, Koen (2018) "Afzien in de Antwerpse cel: niet luchten, geen bezoek en ratten in de gang", *ADNews*. Retrieved from: https://www.ad.nl/buitenland/afzien-in-de-antwerpse-cel-niet-luchten-geen-bezoek-en-ratten-in-de-gang~afc52ea8/?referrer=https%3A%2F%2Fwww.google.com%2F

World Prison Brief (2023) "Belgium", Institute for Crime & Justice Policy Research, February. Retrieved from: https://www.prisonstudies.org/country/belgium

ABOUT THE AUTHOR

Luk Vervaet studies prison abolition and penal politics.

CSC's Corporate Culture is The Fundamental Problem
George Fraser

As an organization, Correctional Service Canada (CSC) not only fails to correct but, in many cases, actively makes it extremely difficult for correction to occur. Like any large organization, CSC has cultures and sub-cultures that have develop organically when human beings gather and particularly when individuals with common purpose begin working together. The 'Blue Wall' correctional culture dominates all others, because it runs in the veins of this hierarchical bureaucratic organization. The 'Blue Wall' culture has no start and no end – it is endemic and it is in-bred.

From personal experience, observations, and what I have read in watchdog reports, as well as recent published books, it is apparent that CSC's 'Blue Wall' culture is at the heart of everything that is wrong. The 'Blue Wall' culture is the lowest common denominator reason as to why CSC is failing to meet its obligations to federally sentenced prisoners, including its obligations to uphold their human rights.

This is not just my opinion, but also the expert opinion of a retired CSC Deputy Warden with 30 years experience in the trenches. He asserts, "the culture is largely responsible for most of the problems that occur within our prisons!" (Clark, 2017, p. 16). There exists "a culture of collective indifference towards both the prisoners and CSC's stated higher goals" (ibid). 'Goals' is in reference to *Correctional and Conditional Release Act* (CCRA) sections 3(a) and 3(b) mandate, and nothing is going to change until there is a seismic organization shift at the top.

One only has to read the February 2019 *Interim Report – Study on the Human Rights of Federally Sentence Persons* by the Standing Senate Committee on Human Rights to understand the depth and scope of the challenges faced by prisoners because CSC is failing to meet its obligations to them. Everything indicates that CSC has been an abject failure to perform their CCRA section 3(a) "safe and humane custody" and section 3(b) "rehabilitation of offenders ... through the provision of programs" objectives.

The following are just some of the issues identified by that Senate Committee on Human Rights Interim Report: inadequate access to health care; inadequate health and dental care; insufficient admission to gradual and structured release; deficient correctional programs, the one-size-fits-all programs are inadequate; poor conditions of confinement; poor access to remedial measures; substandard quantity and quality of food; CSC policies often discriminate against Indigeneity, race, gender, disability, mental health, ethnicity, religion, age, language, sexual orientation, and gender identity in violation of section 3 of the *Canadian Human Rights Act*; pervasive anti-Black and anti-Indigenous racism and discrimination; Indigenous and Black persons have difficulty accessing culturally relevant programming; poor living conditions; prisoners are being charged exorbitant prices for personal purchases; failure to prepare prisoners for release in a timely manner; no systemic access to palliative care; a static security focused approach to mental health rather than therapeutic interventions; lack of post-secondary educational opportunities represent lost opportunities; as well as failure to recognize international human rights standards related to the Nelson Mandela Rules and the Bangkok Rules.

Key to everything that is wrong can be directly attributed to "an organizational culture that sees ... support and services for prisoners as privileges instead of rights" (RIDR, 2019, p. 22).[1] Therein lies the fundamental premise of the Standing Senate Committee on Human Rights study, which asserts "the rights of all human beings must be respected, regardless of who they are. A rights based approach to corrections is vital to ensure that our criminal justice system is fair, equal and effective" (ibid, p. 10).

The Correctional Investigator reports that: a) The 'Blue Wall' "culture remains highly insular", where "learning and critical self-reflection do not come easily" (Zinger, 2018, p. 30); b) Mistreatment of prisoners and human rights abuses result when "problematic elements of organizational culture generates adverse impacts for those under CSC's care and custody" (Zinger, 2017, p. 4); c) "Rehabilitation and reintegration cannot be accomplished in a workplace that tolerates a culture of indifference or impunity" (ibid, p. 4); d) "Openness and transparency are not well ingrained in the CSC organizational culture" (ibid, p. 43); and e) "The culture and infrastructure of corrections has hardened – there have not been progressive changes in the profession" (ibid, p. 5).

Another significant cultural insight for me came after reading the article, "What makes CSC employees happy at work?" in the CSC *Let's Talk Express* publication dated 16 April 2018. My most significant take away from this article concerning CSC employee happiness was that the majority of CSC respondents from across the country derived their employment happiness and satisfaction from their social interaction with their colleagues on the job. While there were a few laudable exceptions, by far and away the majority did not equate and derive happiness and job satisfaction from their actual job assignment or their job performance – their primary reason for being an employee of CSC. The following are some representative and noteworthy happiness and satisfaction samples from respondents that have a direct correlation to their immersion in the 'Blue Wall' culture:

> "The key to having a happy professional life isn't the work you do but the people you work with"; "Lunch with co-workers, spending an hour away from your desk to talk about each other (not work) and learn from each other's backgrounds, likes, dislikes and sharing laughs and dreams etc" (it does not get more dysfunctional than this when the high point of this CSC employees day is lunch); "It's the support and care that fellow employees show each other"; " I have one constant source of happiness, and that is my colleagues"; "We are family"; "Happiness is a group of great co-workers"; "Everyone has each other's back!" (this mentality is at the heart of the 'Blue Wall' culture's Code of Silence).

Something is wrong in the CSC corporate culture where the majority happiness job satisfaction quotient is social and collegial. The "We're all in this together" and "Everyone has each other's back!" mentality is opposed to a job description that is 'functional'. These happiness survey responses show that "too few prison employees care about the prisoners under their care".

My understanding of the 'Blue Wall' culture comes from first and foremost my firsthand experience as a prisoner in Canada's prison system in which prisoner human rights abuse is rampant. While the examples are many, I will mention only a few that are significant to the CSC culture that places a low value on prisoners.

The first is a case of geriatric human rights abuse. Where I am located, at Bath Institution, 50 percent of the prisoner population is about 50 years old. Bath is the epicentre and prima facie of CSC's failure to both recognize and accommodate the senior prisoner demography. Consider that CSC "still has no national strategy to address the health concerns of ¼ of the total inmate population that is now age 50 or older" (Sapers, 2016, p. 12). On a daily basis at Bath Institution, I see prisoners with wheelchairs, walkers, and canes waiting in a medication queue for up to 40 minutes outside on a sidewalk and roadway with no protection from the elements. This winter there have been days with wind chill factors of -40°C. By any civility measure, requiring seniors to wait outside in the elements for up to 40 minutes is a human rights violation that would never be tolerated in any Canadian community. CSC gets away with it because there are no external eyes watching. Bath Institution's health care professionals are complicit bystanders to this human rights injustice and some exacerbate the queue time wait with unnecessary policy enforcement. It is all about the correctional culture's value judgement of prisoners, that they 'lack value' as human beings, and nobody cares if they wait outside in freezing temperatures with no protection from the elements.

A second example stems from 30 August 2019 while I was on an Escorted Temporary Absence (ETA) to the Hotel Dieu Hospital in Kingston for a colonoscopy. Both my escorting officers had their cell phones out and in use while I was laying on a bed, stripped down to hospital garb, in the Gastroenterology intake department, as well as in the operating room while I was undergoing my colonoscopy surgical procedure. Not only did the CSC escorting officers use of their cell phones a breach on my medical confidentiality and privacy, but it is also a breach of hospital policy, because cell phone use is not permitted in patient care areas and around medical equipment. So, that question begs, why would my escorting correctional officers think that having their cell phone camera lens pointed in my direction while I was being prepped for surgery, and then pointed at my sphincter while the colonoscopy procedure was being performed in the operating room, is acceptable behaviour? Easy answer: It is the 'Blue Wall' correctional culture and the value the 'Blue Wall' culture places on prisoners! Blue wall culture transcends individual officer's personal values.

Beyond firsthand experience, I also draw knowledge from what I read in public watch dog reports by both the Correctional Investigator and the Auditor General of Canada. The Correctional Investigator's annual reports continue to report ongoing CSC budget cuts for short-term gain in every sector from Health Care, Food Services, Library Services, and on and on. The recent series of sweeping business transformation decisions to reduce costs by centralizing services that would include: amalgamation / clustering of institutional services; realignment of case management activity; and realignment of resources within treatment centres. These changes were done in many cases "without support by evidence and no demonstrable link to increased public safety" (Sapers, 2015, p. 4). Year after year, the Correctional Investigator's Annual Report can be summed up as such: "There appears to be no end to the issues that quite properly belong with or have been created by CSC maladministration" (Zinger, 2017, p. 7) due to "problematic elements of organizational culture that generates adverse impacts for those under CSC's care and custody" (ibid, p. 4).

In Auditor General reports (Auditor General of Canada, 2003), I read that the office considers parole officers and their managers to be not trained well enough to do their job properly and this skill deficit, critical to a prisoner's rehabilitation and re-entry, has resulted in people being held behind bars longer than they otherwise would be. It does not get more dysfunctional than this! Warehousing prisoners represents job protection for the 'Blue Wall' culture. Parole officers coming from a correctional background are bad news for any prisoner assigned to them due to their 'Blue Wall' indoctrination that prisoners lack human value. Their mentality is to keep prisoners in at the highest security level. Their 'Blue Wall' low enthusiasm and low expectations for prisoners is psychologically damaging to any prisoner to whom they are assigned. I know this from personal experience!

Recent book publications such as *Down Inside: Thirty Years in Canada's Prison Service* by Robert Clark (2017) also shed light on CSC's 'Blue Wall' culture. The author worked in seven different CSC institutions, ending his career as a Deputy Warden. The following are significant quotations germane to the 'Blue Wall' culture.

> Too few prison employees care about the prisoners under their care, other than to make sure they are alive and behaving. Any interest in prisoner's well-being and their chances for becoming Jaw-abiding citizens is almost non-existent (Clark, 2017, p. 16).

> Some prison employees seem to regard the prisoners as less than human and feel it acceptable to mistreat them in myriad ways they would not even consider outside the prison and that they would be ashamed to have their family and friends see (ibid, p. 16).

> Some employees engage in acts that would be a crime outside the prison walls. Many more of these acts are simply crimes of the conscience: racism, verbal and emotional abuse intimidation (ibid, p. 16).

The Senate Committee heard reports where correctional staff had counselled suicide, which is a criminal offence, by telling prisoners who told them that they were feeling suicidal, "Go ahead, commit suicide, it'll be one less person for us to look after" (RIDR, 2019, p. 57). Here at Bath Institution, one geriatric prisoner with stage-4 cancer was counselled to "take the needle" (in reference to MAID) by his doctor and parole officer, ostensibly as a cost saving measure. "The 'Blue Wall' is an overdeveloped sense of solidarity, a level of cohesiveness that transcends one's personal values" (Clark, 2017, p. 17). So-called good correctional officers regularly do bad things, such as engage in "racism, verbal, and emotional abuse, [and] intimidation" that they would never consider engaging in beyond the prison walls where their community, family, and friends could see them. They feel free to participate in "racism, verbal, and emotional abuse, [and] intimidation" within the insular prison walls because they know their secrets are protected by the 'Blue Wall' culture's 'Code of Silence'. "Once immersed in the correctional culture... many staff become loyal to the 'Blue Wall'", while "Many prison staff, no matter their job and no matter their background, begin to see the prisoners as something less than real people" (ibid).

I have seen firsthand what Clark (2017) reports, whereby new 'contract' support staff "start out eager to make a difference in prisoners' lives, only to later fall in with... the 'Blue Wall' culture" that pulls them into the prevailing mindset that "prisoners are unworthy of their time and energy" (ibid). Psychological leveraging by the prevailing culture is a major consideration for any new employee in any organization, because the need for acceptance is basic human nature. New employees want to be accepted by their peers, while their ability to integrate into the corporate culture is also key to both their continued employment and potential consideration for future promotions.

Justice Louise Arbour encountered the 'Blue Wall' when she led the inquiry into the practices of the Prison for Women in 1996. Commenting on Justice Arbour's inquiry, Clark (2017, p. 17), notes: "The deplorable defensive culture that manifested itself during the inquiry has old, established roots within the correctional service... It would seem they are simply entrenched in it". I also watched CPAC rebroadcasts of the Senate's Standing Committee on Human Rights, in which retired CSC Warden staff talked experiences within the CSC culture's 'Blue Wall' code of silence involving bullying, racism, xenophobia, threats, and harassment including vehicle keying and tires flattened over perceived 'Blue Wall' Code of Silence violations.

In reflecting upon CSC cultural, I am reminded of Ashley Smith's death in 2007 and the Coroner's recommendations (114 in all) that came out in 2014. Most of those recommendations focused on the mental health of prisoners subject to federal corrections, yet "most of those recommendations have not been answered individually much less substantively" (Sapers, 2016, p. 17). Avoidance of the Coroner's recommendations was to be expected when one considers that then Commissioner, Don Head, did everything possible to avoid testifying at the Ashley Smith Coroner's Inquest. Consider this avoidance of "doing the right things for the right reasons" due to the correctional code of silence and be aware that this person was the Commissioner of CSC.

There are also lessons to be drawn from the preventable death of Matthew Hines on 26 May 2015. The circumstances and events that give rise to avoidable deaths in the Canadian prison system are not isolated, but rather are systemic and pervasive in nature. It is all about the Blue Wall culture in which "some prison employees seem to regard the prisoners as less than human and feel it acceptable to mistreat them in myriad ways" (Clark, 2017, p. 16).

In another case, "the body of a deceased inmate 21 was removed from his cell and left uncovered in the hallway for three and a half hours before the police and coroner arrived on the scene to investigate. Officers stood watch and walked over the body while conducting rounds" (ibid, p. 24).

A word about corporate culture is also in order to understand what the 'Blue Wall' is: the way things get done; the personality of the organization, the shared beliefs, values, norms, and behaviour of the group; and shared basic assumptions individuals have to succeed in an organization. "The only trustworthy predictor of on-the-job success, for an individual, is how closely an individual's work habits match the organizational culture" (Gilles, 2000). For any employee, their continued employment and happiness quotient in an organization depends on their ability to integrate into the corporate culture. Think of the Robert Clark (2017) statement, "The 'Blue Wall' is an overdeveloped sense of solidarity, a level of cohesiveness that transcends one's personal values" (Sapers, 2016, p. 17), and how it relates to the aforementioned response to that CSC happiness survey, "Everyone has each other's back!" These concepts are at the heart of the 'Blue Wall' culture's code of silence.

Within CSC, there is not a single culture but an integration of multiple cultures. While the 'Blue Wall' culture is the dominant culture that is pervasive throughout the organization, there are many sub-cultures that form the basis for silos in the organization. Sub-cultures may share certain characteristics, norms, values, and beliefs, or be totally different. Within CSC, these subcultures function cooperatively with the dominant 'Blue Wall' for the most part, because the 'Blue Wall' culture sets the organization tone and demeanour in 'the way things get done'. Any new prisoner policy initiative, whether coming from the institutional level or the Commissioner's office, is always presented to the Union of Canadian Correctional Officers executive for their consideration and input before implementation into the prisoner population. In other words, the Blue Wall's support is necessary for CSC to achieve its strategic goals.

Corporate culture is not the ideals, vision, and mission laid out in the corporation's mission statement. Rather, it is expressed in the day-to day practices, communications, and beliefs. Leadership does not create corporate culture, but it can shape it. Whenever human beings gather, and particularly when individuals with a common purpose begin working together, thinking processes will develop and an organizational culture will be created. While 'culture' is invisible, it is the dominant player in any organization's bottom line performance. Corporate culture creates 'shared values' by the group that are unseen and latent. However, they are deeply embedded in the organization's and individual's behaviour(s). Because corporate culture is not 'official', it functions as a hidden mechanism of coordination directing each individual toward the common goal. The mission of an organizational culture is not necessarily in the overall interests of the organization (e.g. the 'Blue Wall').

In many cases, the causes of problems in an organization (i.e. profitability, performance, responsiveness to issues, personality, and attitudes as well as, in CSC's case, the perception that prisoners have low value as justification for human rights violations) relate to an organization's structure, leadership, or the employees themselves, and are directly related to the culture and sub-cultures of an organization. Within CSC, the 'Blue Wall' transcends individual personal values at all levels of the organization, including the Commissioner's office. For any organization to attain its strategic 'official' objectives, it must understand if the dominant culture supports its strategic goals (Hagberg and Heifetz, 2000). "The forces of corporate culture" at the macro, the micro, and individual levels "are powerful because they operate outside our awareness" (Schein, 2013, p. 18). For any bureaucratic organization such as CSC, culture issues are especially difficult to address because of the lack of sophisticated leading edge human resource management, along with the fact that bottom line profitability and performance is always sloughed off as the result of some externality (i.e. government policy, other criminal justice system players etc.) that are beyond their control.

In what follows, I present a few instances when a corporate culture needs to be changed (think CSC). First, when an organization has been around for so long its way of working becomes so entrenched that it is hindering the entity from adapting to changes. Second, when the staff believe their sole purpose for working is to collect a paycheque and a pension after 25 years. I have asked multiple staff (i.e. support staff, health care, correctional officers, and even a parole officer) "What possible job satisfaction do you get working in a prison?" and, inevitably, the answers is "A paycheque and a pension after 30 years!" I then follow-up with, "That's no Quality of Work Life (QWL) ... After retiring, you will end up being a worse person than when you came in!" Third, when staff think "the key to having a happy professional life isn't the work you do but the people you work with" and "lunch with co-workers" is the high point of the workday.

Trying to salvage a broken dysfunctional system is both poorly conceived and wasteful. Here are the problems I see. First, CSC does not have a clear purpose. While they are mandated to and purport to rehabilitate and reintegrate prisoners, because of budgetary constraints and public pressure, those functions are often neglected and replaced by warehousing. Second, the Commissioner's office desperately clings to the 'status quo' and pussy foots around the 'Blue Wall's' correctional tribal culture. The performance of the current CSC management structure is totally unacceptable where recidivism is concerned. Third, CSC's failure to perform their most important mandate to this level is simply cheating prisoners out of opportunities to successfully reintegrate. In fact, all criminal justice system stakeholders, including Canadian taxpayers, are being cheated by the 'abject' performance failure(s) of CSC. Fourth, there is no national strategy for senior prisoners. As the Office of the Correctional Investigator put it in 2019, "The conditions of confinement of older individuals in federal custody are lacking in terms of personal safety and dignity, and the prospect of these individuals returning to the community is often neglected and overlooked, all of which jeopardizes the protection of their human rights". The findings of this investigative report show that CSC's treatment of older offenders in federal custody does not respect their human rights, or "is not justified in terms of institutional security or public safety; is inconsistent with the administration of lawful sentences imposed by courts, and: is unnecessarily costly to Canadians" (OCI and CHRC, 2019, p. 2). Both the Department of Public Safety and Correctional Service Canada have been complicit bystanders to the "systemic discrimination" of aging and elderly prisoners in Canadian penitentiaries.

It is imperative that the Standing Senate Committee on Human Rights recommend a CSC audit along the lines of the RCMP report conducted by the former Auditor General, Sheila Fraser. Such an audit would address the 'cultural' issues due to the remarkable similarities between both the RCMP and CSC. Statements made in that RCMP report would equally apply to CSC: "Lack of Ministry oversight"; "Hierarchical top down organization that has proven resistant to change"; "Expertise needed to modernize the administration"; "Leadership seems incapable of implementing change"; "Not capable of making the broad systemic changes of its own accord"; "Not a state unto itself"; "Leadership is not capable of making the necessary systemic changes of its own accord"; "Need for an overarching and radical change in governance"; "Need for 'cultural' change" (MacCharles, 2017). It is time for CSC shake up with a total 180-degree paradigm shift for 21st century relevancy.

As Senator Runciman once said, "the only way we're going to see significant change is change in staffing at the senior levels in CSC". This is echoed by Robert Clark when he says "many of the people at the top will not risk poor relations with staff or the unions in order to ensure every prisoners' rights are respected" (Clark, 2017, p. 17).

What a Correctional Service Canada 180-degree paradigm shift requires is a Board of Management comprised of skilled professionals with a proven track record from academia and the private sector. This is the only organization model that has any chance of making the necessary changes for CSC to become 21st century relevant. A Board of Management would have no allegiance or ties to the existing tribal culture(s). They would have no parochial protectionism for heritage policy that has failed to deliver and they would be able to build an organizational framework that is open to innovation and driven by collaboration with experts and boards of advisors.

It should not be surprising that the best managed Canadian businesses would have something to teach CSC about Human Resource Management, starting with an expansion and strengthening the employment applicant pool. CSC needs to start attracting the best in their fields and not just people looking for a default career with a pension. This is especially important for correctional officers who end up within the service because they have been unsuccessful in obtaining employment in their first and second career choices. Additionally, nepotism is not serving CSC well, because it feeds into the 'Blue Wall' culture of entitlement and cronyism. The under-performers protected by the unions need to be fired.

While it may be a stretch for some, any new cultural paradigm must consider prisoners to be human. If prisoners can be seen as human beings with value, as potential law-abiding citizens, this would be a huge and necessary 21st century hurdles, to validate prisoner identity as other than 'criminal'. Prisoners want to be respected for their potential value. They want to be collaboratively engaged in meaningful rehabilitation programs and re-training (OAG, 2015). They want to successfully reintegrate back into society. They want to live a life with purpose. None of this is possible with the current CSC Commissioner's office administration. They have had their chance and they continue to trip, fall, and stumble because they are tainted by the 'Blue Wall' culture. Most Commissioner office staff have arrived at their present lofty position after successive promotions within the ranks, and they have been successful because individuals succeed in an organization by aligning themselves with the corporate culture. The Commissioner, Deputy Commissioners, and Assistant Commissioners are all proof positive that "the only trustworthy predictor of on-the-job success, for an individual, is how closely an individual's work habits match the organizational culture" (Gilles, 2000, n.p.). They are all tainted by the 'Blue Wall' culture, even if they do not recognize that fact because the forces of corporate culture at the macro, the micro, and individual levels operate outside our awareness. A Board of Management without the encumbrance of stale and inept recycled leadership failures provides the best management structure to execute and deliver transparency and accountability to deliver bottom line conformance to the CSC mandate under section 3(b) of the CCRA, which involves "assisting the rehabilitation of offenders and their reintegration into the community – through the provision of programs" to 21st century relevancy. A Board of Management would have no allegiance to "the culture that is largely responsible for most of the problems that occur within our prisons" (Clark, 2017, p. 16). Everything contained in the foregoing is my "thoughts, beliefs and opinions" (Government of Canada, 1982) based on my personal experience and observations.

ENDNOTE

[1] Marie-Claude Landry, Chief Commissioner of the Canadian Human Rights Commission as reported in the *Interim Report of the Standing Senate Committee on Human Rights*, p. 22.

REFERENCE

Clark, Robert (2017) *Down Inside: Thirty Years in Canada's Prison Service*, Fredericton: Goose Lane Editions.

Correctional Service Canada [CSC] (2010) *Section 2: The Mandate, Mission and Priorities of the Correctional Service of Canada*, Ottawa.

Giles, Russ (2000) Identifying and Influencing Organizational Culture [Electronic version] / R. Giles. Retrieved from: http://www.informanet.com

Government of Canada (1982) *Constitution Act, Canadian Charter of Rights and Freedoms, section 2(b)*.

Hagberg, Richard and Julie Heifetz (2000) "Corporate Culture / Organizational Culture: Understanding and Assessment". Retrieved from: http://www.hcgnet.com/html/articles/understanding-Culture/html

MacCharles, Tonda (2017) "Two new reports urge radical reform of how the RCMP is managed", *Toronto Star* – May 15. Retrieved from: https://www.thestar.com/news/canada/2017/05/15/mounties-are-incapable-of-policing   themselves-rcmp-watchdog-report-says.html

Office of the Correctional Investigator [OCI] and Canadian Human Rights Commission [CHRC] (2019) *Aging and Dying in Prison: An Investigation into the Experiences of Older Individuals in Federal Custody* – February 28, Ottawa: Office of the Correctional Investigator.

Office of the Auditor General of Canada [OAG] (2015) "Report 6 Preparing Male Offenders for Release – Correctional Service Canada", *Reports of the Auditor General of Canada* – May 3, Ottawa: Office of the Auditor General of Canada.

Office of the Auditor General of Canada [OAG] (2003) "Chapter Four, Correctional Service of Canada: Reintegration of Male Offenders", *Reports of the Auditor General of Canada* – May 7, Ottawa: Office of the Auditor General of Canada.

Sapers, Howard (2016) *Office of the Correctional Investigator Annual Report 2015-2016* – June 30, Ottawa: Office of the Correctional Investigator.

Sapers, Howard (2015) *Office of the Correctional Investigator Annual Report 2014-2015* – June 26, Ottawa: Office of the Correctional Investigator.

Schein, Edgar (2013) *Humble Inquiry: The Gentle Art of Asking Instead of Telling*, Oakland: Berrett-Koehler Publishers.

Schein, Edgar (2010) *Organizational Culture and Leadership* (Volume 2), New York: John Wiley & Sons.

Standing Senate Committee on Human Rights [RIDR] (2019) *Interim Report* – February, Ottawa: Senate of Canada.

Zinger, Ivan (2018) *Office of the Correctional Investigator Annual Report 2017-2018* – June 29, Ottawa: Office of the Correctional Investigator.

Zinger, Ivan (2017) *Office of the Correctional Investigator Annual Report 2016-2017* – June 28, Ottawa: Office of the Correctional Investigator.

ABOUT THE AUTHOR

George Fraser is currently imprisoned at Bath Institution.

Restoring Our Honour from Gangs to the Garrison
Shon Pernice

"Our objective here at the Missouri Veterans Program is to reduce recidivism in the veteran community by restoring our honour and means to succeed. We will accomplish this objective by providing veteran specific resources and a therapeutic environment".

– MVP Mission Statement

Service in the United States military can develop lifelong qualities and characteristics in an individual. The main mission of the armed forces is to serve and protect its citizens so that they may live in a healthy environment. While many veterans struggle with a variety of social problems, and some end up in prison, their warrior values can be revived when a challenge becomes an opportunity. The men residing in the Veterans Wing at the Moberly Correctional Center (MCC) were posed with such a challenge when, as a last-ditch effort to help, a struggling non-veteran was assigned to their housing unit. This was a trial for the institution's administration, the veterans, and a young man who became a product of the prison system at an early age.

While growing up, Jimmy Steps moved frequently around the neighbourhoods of Kansas City, Missouri. At the age of 14, he entered into the juvenile system and was then arrested for second-degree murder and armed criminal action at 17. By his nineteenth birthday, Steps was placed in a maximum-security prison where hardened prisoners sized him up on a daily basis.

While trying to survive in the volatile environment, he was charged with voluntary manslaughter after being attacked by another prisoner and defending his own life. For most teens in adult institutions, they become either predator or prey. As a result, Steps joined a prison gang. Although he had experimented with drugs before incarceration, he became addicted to heroin while in prison. When that was not available, he would use anything that would get him high. Steps states that, "I became a junkie in prison". His drug use was a "coping device" and a "way to pass the time". Whenever drugs are involved, criminal behaviours and criminal thinking are magnified. Narcotics and gang affiliation became the main source of power, money, and enjoyment for him.

Steps arrived at MCC in the summer of 2018 due to his custody level being lowered by the prison administration. It was going to be a fresh start for Steps. However, the criminal mindset was programmed into his way of thinking. Drug use, fights, and gang life were the tenets of his religion, purpose, and understanding of normalcy. Steps explains that, "Old habits die hard", as he began accumulating so many conduct violations that he was going to be levelled back up to a maximum-security prison. The official reason was listed as, "Poor institutional adjustment". However, some staff members had an ounce of hope left for Steps and wanted to try a different plan of action as a last resort – it was a plan that could potentially backfire and thereby create a disturbance among the prisoner population. In July 2021, Steps was assigned to the Missouri Veterans Program at MCC.

Now picture a six-foot tall male with prison tattoos on his face, neck, arms, and most of his body, along with a cast on his right arm from his last fight, come strolling into the most quiet and disciplined wing at the institution. Most of the veterans did not know who Steps was due to his gang association and because he had spent the last several months in administrative segregation (the hole). Fear, anger, and resentment hit many of the veterans like a tidal wave. However, some of the veterans knew Steps from the prison yard and welcomed him into their environment. This was their chance to lead by example and expose Steps to military values such as strength, honour, and professionalism, something that Steps never had as a foundation in his life. Now, the veterans had an opportunity to once again serve a member of society. They were presented with a person who would one day be released back into the community, but still needed direction and values to be set by example.

After living in a military-style environment with more rules, standards, and requirements than the rest of the prison system, it was time for me to sit down and ask Steps some questions about his experience. It had been 30 days since his arrival into the Veterans Wing and the tensions surrounding this civilian among the vets had sharply decreased. To live in the esteemed Veterans Wing, Steps had additional restrictions set by the prison administration to see if his "old habits" would reemerge. Therefore, I asked Steps how he felt on his first day in the wing and he replied, "I felt nervous about the Veterans Wing. I was thrown into an element that I knew nothing about". Steps was required to take the two-week mandatory Orientation Class, the Core Values class, and the Colour Guard course. All residents of the Veterans Wing are required to participate in the flag raising and lowering ceremony. Steps adapted impressively to the military-style leadership positions that govern the daily operations of the wing. I inquired about how he was able to conform to this garrison-type configuration, he replied:

The structure we live by in the wing is no different than the (prison) yard. The gang affiliations have a ranking system adopted by the military. I knew who I was accountable to and who was accountable to me. But this ranking system (Veterans Wing) is for the positive, not the negative. I understand the ranking structure in the Veterans Wing and I respect it.

Since Steps was able to remain at this institution and has modified his behaviour, he is now eligible for the offender long-term drug treatment program. He is currently on the transfer list and is eagerly awaiting his next challenge. Steps described having an "awakening moment" in the Veterans Wing, which allowed him to realize that "prison is only temporary", and that a good life is possible for him outside of these fences. He confesses that his "missing foundations in life were built upon criminality, narcotics, and misery".

I asked Steps what he had learned so far in our wing and he admirably described how he has discovered a different type of people to emulate, ask for advice, and from whom to seek knowledge. These are men who had built a foundation while they were in the military service, a foundation that Steps missed out on. Upon concluding the interview, Steps looked at me with a grateful smile and reported that, "This was the best four weeks I've spent in prison". While this second chance for Steps is still in its infancy, the experience is a validation for the veterans in the wing that reflects "You can take the man out of the military, but not the military out of the man". Bravo Zulu! (Navy term for Good Job).

ABOUT THE AUTHOR

Shon Pernice is currently imprisoned. He can be reached at the following address:

Shon Pernice 1236421
HU 4C-990
Moberly Correctional Center
5201 S. Morley Street
Moberly, Missouri 65270
USA

Changing Directions
Darris Drake Jr

As I stare at my door which rarely opens, the reality of solitary confinement weighs heavily upon my shoulders. Is this rehabilitation? There are days when I do not hear my own voice and, as days pass, I find myself more frequently answering my own mental contemplations. Without a strong mind, one can easily tumble into a mental crisis. That is a regular occurrence around here, evident by the screams of desperation, followed by the frantic kicks and punches which rattle the same doors at which I am staring. The unbudging steel fuelling the flames of helplessness, charring their resolve.

Somehow this environment is not alien to me. It is by far not the highlight of my existence, rather it has become a minor inconvenience. Writing those last two words was not easy – to say that the loss of my freedom is a minor convenience exposes my institutionalization. I have spent a lifetime in cells just like this one and, when I was free, the desperation was still present. After the life I lived, immersed in the criminal subculture, things like desperation, violence, drug addiction, resentment, greed, and death became my social norms. To experience anything outside of that was alien.

I have never valued societal norms or felt included in normative society, so my transition to the subculture was a seamless one. I think most people mistakenly assume that everyone knows and understands the societal norms, and should therefore abide by them. However, when you are not provided the stability to develop your own values and a platform to pursue them, then societal norms become chains of oppression. I always felt that society was impressing its will upon me, and as a child I had no way to express this feeling, so I rebelled. As an adolescent, anytime I felt an authority (whether institutional or parental), I began to fight that noose and thrash against it.

That feeling of helplessness was the source of my anger. Not knowing how to fight it, I began to physically impose my will, whether on my peers or anyone in whom I perceived weakness. I used aggression to hide the scared, insecure child I really was. I have harmed a lot of people running from those feelings of helplessness, some of whom I love.

Two years ago, I made the decision to change my life. Deep down, I did not believe it was possible. My experiences caused me to develop a low sense of self-worth. I began to educate myself and take some painful trips down memory lane to find the root causes of my behaviour. Learning how to heal from the inside-out has been a priceless tool on my journey. Though there are still times, such as this, where my intellect does not apply and my aggression is still waiting in the background. It is a process, of which I will always have to be aware.

I am in the process of getting an associate's degree in Human Services and would like to get a bachelor's degree in Criminology. My purpose is to learn what caused my criminal behaviour and help kids so that they do not have to struggle the same way I have. I am serving 236 months for first degree assault. If I can help kids find themselves before they experience this, I will be fulfilled.

ABOUT THE AUTHOR

Darris Drake Jr. is currently imprisoned. He can be reached at the following address:

Darris Drake Jr. #871756
F-B-11
Strafford Creek Correction Center
191 Constantine Way
Aberdeen, WA 98520
USA

A Look at Prison Overcrowding from the Inside
David Fleenor

Analyzing the problem of prison overcrowding led the Council of State Governments (CSG Justice Center) to presume that the enactment of Oklahoma's 85% law would cause dangerous levels of prison overcrowding as "[v]iolent offenders [would be] serving longer sentences in prison than ever before".[1] This is simply not true. Had the CSG Justice Center conducted in-person meetings with people currently inside corrections, they would have discovered that: 1) prior to the enactment of the 85% law, people convicted of crimes classified as violent have and are currently serving the longest prison sentences in Oklahoma's history; and 2) the Pardon and Parole Board's unwillingness to pass applicants who have served 25 consecutive calendar years or more in the Department of Corrections to a stage-two parole and/or commutation hearing is significantly contributing to the problem of prison overcrowding.

People convicted of crimes classified as violent prior to the enactment of the 85% law have, and are currently serving, the longest sentences in Oklahoma's history. To date, the longest consecutive term of incarceration served by a person convicted of a crime classified as violent under the 85% law[2] is 21 years. The longest consecutive term of incarceration served by a person convicted of a crime classified as violent prior to the 85% law is over 50 years.[3] It is an unfortunate truth, but in Oklahoma a person serving 21 consecutive calendar years of incarceration inside the Department of Corrections shocks the conscience of few in this state, not even the incarcerated person or his family.

To better illustrate the point, this writer conducted a survey of the 40 men assigned to the living quarters on D-2-Right at the Joseph Harp Correctional Center on the evening of 28 October 2021. It was discovered that 18 of the 40 men assigned to the housing unit were serving sentences for crimes classified as violent under Oklahoma's 85% law. Collectively, these 18 men had served a total of 229 years in the Department of Corrections at an approximate cost of $3,893,000 to the Oklahoma taxpayer. The remaining 22 men were serving sentences for crimes classified as violent, which were imposed prior to the enactment of the 85% law. Collectively, this group of 22 men had served a total of 708 years in the Department of Corrections at an approximate cost of $12,036,000 to the Oklahoma taxpayer – with no mercy insight! Indeed, the actual cost of incarcerating these 22 men is much higher than estimated in this article, as the majority of them are over 50 years and older, meaning they are prisoners who generally have high health care costs when compared to their younger counterparts.

These figures tend to support the conclusions of several long-term studies[4] that have revealed that merely warehousing people until they die, despite the criminal offense, is not an effective strategy for ensuring public safety. These arbitrary sentencing practices not only significantly contribute to the problem of prison overcrowding, but they are also responsible for the mental and physical deterioration of those who have had to endure a lifetime of hyper-vigilance and hopelessness.

In Oklahoma, the Pardon and Parole Board's unwillingness to pass applicants who have served 25 consecutive years or more in the Department of Corrections to a stage-two parole and/or commutation hearing is significantly contributing to the problem of prison overcrowding. Of the 22 men on my unit that were serving sentences imposed prior to the enactment of the 85% law, all of them expressed feelings of hopelessness and despair because they believe they will die in prison without a meaningful opportunity to prove they no longer pose a threat to public safety. Those feelings stemmed from the Board's unwillingness to look past their commitment offense in deciding whether or not to pass them to stage two.

In Oklahoma, all applicants convicted of crimes classified as violent are reviewed for parole and/or commutation in two-stages. During the initial review, or first-stage, the Parole Board considers only the applicant's commitment offense, or nature of the crime, as the relevant factor in making the decision as to whether or not to pass the applicant to the second stage. Despite strong arguments that commitment offense alone is an insufficient factor in determining suitability for clemency[5] Oklahoma appears to be on the path of excluding a particular category of prisoners from back-end release mechanisms, such as parole and/or commutation, based on that very metric.

Oklahoma only has a part-time Parole Board that meets twice a month on the call of the Chair Person. The purpose of the meeting, in part, is to initially review all scheduled applications for parole and/or commutation on behalf of the Governor. During said meetings, the members of the Board routinely deny approximately 300 applicants without explanation each morning before lunch, which adds up to just over 60 seconds of consideration per application. It is the manifest indifference exhibited by the Board during the performance of a constitutionally prescribed duty that works to effectively repeal the Governor's power to grant clemency to all deemed worthy. Simply stated, it is unconstitutional for the Board to use an incarcerated person's commitment offense as the basis to forever exclude them from the privilege of executive clemency.

Moreover, the law requiring the Board's investigator to compile a report detailing the incarcerated life of the applicant, which is necessary to the "deemed worthy" metric, is not triggered unless the applicant is passed to stage two. Meaning that the vast majority of people, especially those sentenced prior to the enactment of the 85% law, will never be afforded a meaningful opportunity to demonstrate their worthiness of executive clemency because they cannot outlive their commitment offense.

From the outside of corrections looking inward, it is easy to justify the Board's actions during the initial review process as a consequence of its part-time status. However, that perspective becomes distorted when the facts are made clear. A look at the initial review process from the inside of corrections will bring the Board's actions into sharper focus. From this perspective, it is clear that no one convicted in the past 21 years of a crime classified as violent, under the 85% law, has ever appeared on the parole docket of the Board for initial review. The reason is because everyone serving a term-of-year sentence under the 85% law accrues earned credits that are immediately applied to the remaining 15% of their sentence the day they reach the 85% point.

This means two things: 1) every person serving a term-of-year sentence under the 85% law will discharge their sentence the day he or she reaches the 85% point; and 2) the only people placed on the regular parole docket of the Parole Board for "initial review" are those that were sentenced prior to the enactment of the 85% law.

POLICY RECOMMENDATIONS

Major reforms that go far beyond the scope of this article are needed at the Oklahoma Pardon and Parole Board. However, I will make two policy recommendations that I think would have the effect of undermining our State's misguided assumption that the best strategy for ensuring public safety is incarcerating people, without meaningful review, until they die.

First, I recommend a new administrative policy mandating a stage two parole and/or commutation hearing for every incarcerated person after they have served 25 years in the custody of the Oklahoma Department of

Corrections. At a minimum, this would provide at least one meaningful in-person opportunity for an applicant to demonstrate that they have done the necessary work to transform themselves into someone who is willing and able to live within the confines of the law.

Second, I recommend that the Pardon and Parole Board hire a formerly incarcerated person to work as a parole and/or commutation liaison assisting only those incarcerated applicants who have served 25 years or more in the Department of Corrections. This would not only facilitate the process, but it would also bring hope to the hopeless.

ENDNOTES

[1] The Council of State Governments (2012) *Justice Reinvestment in Oklahoma*, page 18.
[2] In 1999, House Bill 1008 created two new sections of law, Title 21 O.S.1999 §§12.1 and 13.1, colloquially known as the 85% law.
[3] Ronald T. Koonce #76423 has been incarcerated in the Oklahoma Department of Corrections since 1967.
[4] Clear, Todd (2009) *Imprisoning Communities: How Mass Incarceration makes Disadvantaged Neighborhoods Worse*, Oxford: Oxford University Press.
[5] Rapaport, Elizabeth (2003) "Straight is the Gate: Capital Clemency in the United States from Gregg to Atkins", *NML Rev.*, 33, 349.

ABOUT THE AUTHOR

David R. Fleenor has served over 25 years on a sentence of life without parole and writes from the Joseph Harp Correctional Center in Oklahoma. He can be reached at the following address:

David R. Fleenor #241218
JHCC
P.O. Box 548 (D-2-118)
Lexington, OK 73051-0548
USA

Reflecting on the Delivery of the Inside-Out Prison Exchange Program During the COVID-19 Pandemic

Dwayne Antojado, Haozhou Sun and Marietta Martinovic

ABSTRACT

The Inside-Out Prison Exchange Program (IOPEP) encompasses university (outside) students and incarcerated (inside) students undertaking a university course alongside each other behind the walls of a prison. In the Australian IOPEP, students are taught *Comparative Criminal Justice Systems*. In 2020, the IOPEP was moved online halfway through the course delivery due to the COVID-19 pandemic to reduce the potential of transmission in prisons. In 2021, in adherence to COVID-19 safety regulations and restrictions in prisons, the IOPEP delivery was also modified by reducing the number of outside students coming into prison. This paper presents Haozhou Sun's reflection of his 2021 IOPEP's learning experience. Although Sun was not able to have the same level of interaction traditionally obtained by IOPEP students, it is clear that the majority of the program's aims were still achieved despite changes in delivery.

WHAT IS THE IOPEP?

The Inside-Out Prison Exchange Program (IOPEP) "is a blended learning program where university (outside) students and incarcerated (inside) students come together as equals in the university context to learn with and from each other, in prison, whilst undertaking a university subject" (Van Grundy et al., 2013 as cited in Martinovic et al., 2018, p. 437). The program was implemented by Dr. Marietta Martinovic from the Royal Melbourne Institute of Technology (RMIT) University in collaboration with Corrections Victoria (Department of Justice and Community Safety) (Martinovic et al., 2018). IOPEP is currently being delivered across six Victorian prisons.

IOPEP was developed in 1997 by Lori Pompa of Temple University and a lifer named Paul Perry at Graterford prison (King et al., 2019). It was subsequently expanded into a training package to enable other higher education providers to facilitate the program (IOPEP Centre, 2017). Up until 2022, over 2000 IOPEP classes have been taught, with more than 60,000 students participating in classes across the USA, Canada, Australia, United Kingdom, and Norway (Inside-Out Centre, 2022).

Students undertaking the Australian IOPEP are taught *Comparative Criminal Justice Systems* (Martinovic et al., 2018), which examines criminal justice systems (CJS) worldwide. All students, inside and outside, are subject to the same learning expectations per university policy and guidelines, including writing three short reflections, preparing and delivering a group presentation on the CJS of a country of their choice, and a major reflective assessment (see Antojado, 2022 for an example). These assessments are then graded as per the standard university marking criteria (Martinovic et al., 2018).

PURPOSE AND IMPACT OF IOPEP

King and colleagues (2019) suggest that IOPEP allows both student groups to critically explore their own beliefs and identities to foster social change and overcome social barriers. Whilst engaging in higher education is the purpose for which students come together in the IOPEP, the aim is much broader, that is, to challenge the stereotypes embedded in society, and start a dialogue which will change policies and thereby improve the CJS. The program also sparks conversations, discussions, and opportunities which challenge deeply embedded societal stereotypes that impinge effective reform efforts. In other words, during the course, outside students see inside students as humans, challenging mainstream stereotypes.

Long and Barnes' (2016) comprehensive evaluation of IOPEP found that all students were able to improve critical thinking skills and were able to critically engage with learning materials. Similarly, other IOPEP related research has shown that when inside students learn with outside students, they increase their ability to engage with educational material (Allred et al., 2013; Hilinski-Rosick and Blackmer, 2014; Hyatt, 2009; Werts, 2013). They are therefore better able to better negotiate their own values and beliefs against the backdrop of growing punitive sentiment in society (Conti, et al., 2013; Hilinski-Rosick and Blackmer, 2014; Martinovic and Liddell, 2019; Antojado et al., 2023).

The IOPEP's pedagogy is based on transformative-dialogic learning, which is reliant upon participants sharing their knowledge and experiences. Dialogue allows active participation as all students self-reflect, explore, and develop an understanding by sharing ideas, critiquing material, and reconciling differences (Butin, 2013). This brings a richer understanding of the complexities faced by people experiencing the criminal justice system

(Pompa, 2002). Furthermore, students begin to reflect on their own values and biases and recognize the inaccuracies of mainstream ideologies within their communities and broader society (Conti et al., 2013; Hilinski-Rosick and Blackmer, 2014; O'Brien et al., 2021; Wyant and Lockwood, 2018). "Walls to Bridges" in Canada, a social justice iteration of the USA's IOPEP program, has very similar purposes and outcomes identified in this section (Pollack, 2019; Pollack and Mayor, 2023).

DOING THE IOPEP
DURING THE COVID-19 PANDEMIC

In 2020, the IOPEP was moved online halfway through its delivery due to the onset of the COVID-19 pandemic to reduce the potential of transmission in prisons. In 2021, following COVID-19 safety regulations and restrictions, the IOPEP was also modified to lessen the risk of COVID-19 transmission. As a result, only five outside students attended the prison learning with 15 inside students simultaneously, whilst the other 10 outside engaged in learning through the online learning space, rotating every three weeks. Despite these modifications due to the pandemic, all 15 outside and 15 inside students met weekly during a semester, enabling students to build rapport and professional relationships with each other. Research has indicated that inside and outside students quickly create a positive and collaborative learning environment that induces knowledge-building through conversations, discussions, and debates (see Martinovic and Liddell, 2020; Martinovic et al., 2018). Inside students share stories about their experiences with the criminal justice system, allowing outside students to gain a deeper understanding of their criminal justice involvement. On the other hand, outside students provide inside students with theoretical knowledge and perspectives that help inside students better understand the system they are first-hand experiencing (see Martinovic and Liddell, 2020; Martinovic et al., 2018).

Martinovic and Liddell (2019) found that students graduating from the IOPEP engendered more compassion and empathy towards those entangled within the criminal justice system. IOPEP facilitated students' change in perception, quashing their preconceived ideas about prisoner stereotypes. Stereotyping prisoners into one homogenous group can have deleterious effects on the efforts of the penal estate in carrying out its rehabilitative objectives, particularly when these stereotypes impinge on a practitioner's ability to carry out its duties professionally without bias (Martinovic et al., 2018). As outside students graduate and enter the criminal justice field professionally, they need to understand the complexity of criminal justice involvement, not just from knowledge derived through academic theorizing, but also from the lived experiences of potential future clients (see Martinovic and Liddell, 2019).

The modified structure of the program in 2020 impacted the dynamics of the student group, mainly as outside students attended the prison in small groups and only for three sessions throughout the entire course. Students had to repeat the process of getting to know each other every three weeks. This process of the program is perhaps the most awkward and anxiety-provoking period for all students (Martinovic et al., 2018). Outside students usually come into the prison espousing preconceived ideas about prisoners, often in an unpropitious light. Inside students enter the program space expecting to be embarrassed or stereotyped (Martinovic and Liddell, 2019). The process of undoing the prejudices both outside and inside students espoused as a consequence of negative public discourses about prisoners takes time, usually a few sessions. However, by the time both student cohorts felt comfortable, outside students returned to the online learning environment, while inside students were reintroduced to a new outside student group. Thus, it is likely that both student cohorts were less willing to vocalize their views and opinions and share their experiences of the CJS.

Despite its modified structure, the offering of the IOPEP was still beneficial to both inside and outside students, as is evident in the reflection of Haozhou Sun below. The COVID-19 pandemic has changed the way prisoners live in prisons, generally in ways which exacerbate the experience of subjugation. For example, solitary confinement is used as a measure to isolate incoming prisoners, as well as those believed to have contracted or be in contact with a person believed to have been exposed to the coronavirus. The detrimental effects of solitary confinement to those held in custody (particularly on mental health) are well established in the literature (e.g. Metzner and Fellner, 2010). However, it seems that COVID-19 will remain in our society for quite some time, including its less desirable features requiring people to abstain from close interaction. IOPEP will therefore need to continually adapt to prisons' highly transient and bureaucratic nature, whilst still trying to ensure fidelity to its objectives. This is a difficult task and one that may well need a few trials to perfect.

HAOZHOU SUN'S REFLECTION OF DOING THE IOPEP

The IOPEP has challenged my understanding of the CJS, particularly the function of its three arms: police, courts, and corrections. My participation in this program has also pushed me to think critically about contemporary issues related to the criminal justice system. I learned a great deal about restorative justice and alternative sentencing approaches – things I did not even know existed. I also now understand the importance of therapeutic sanctions which help facilitate one's reintegration back into society, which is quite difficult for many released prisoners.

When I first arrived at Ravenhall Correctional Centre, I was pleasantly surprised. The jail was depicted as a scary, dark, evil place when I watched it on television. Movies and television shows regularly featured iron bars and solitary spaces. However, when I entered this jail for the first time, I saw a big oval with colourful buildings all around. I almost thought I had arrived at a university or high school campus. I felt amazed at how this place is so different compared to my initial perception. During my first interaction with the outside students, they had the same curiosities as I did when they first arrived here. They were inquisitive about our accommodation, the level of freedom we were provided, and the type of food/cuisine given to us by the prison. I was glad the outside students showed interest in better understanding the "real life" conditions of prison, something they would not have otherwise been exposed to had they not been a part of IOPEP.

At Ravenhall prison, individuals can choose to participate in various educational courses and rehabilitative programs. I think that this is a very humane and efficient way to focus on a prisoner's rehabilitation. Some of the main reasons people come to jail are because of complex needs, mental health issues, substance abuse disorders, and anger management problems. Providing treatment for these mediating factors to crime is therefore relevant in a person's rehabilitation pathways and, in some ways, IOPEP provides this through normalized dialogue with people outside the criminal justice space. Education is a great way to develop an openness to future pathways and possibly gain employment. It can also decrease the reoffending rate by providing criminalized people with employment opportunities that reduce the likelihood of future criminal involvement. I have seen a lot of men in this prison who have a positive motivation to change but do not know how. I always encourage them to sign up for some of the programs and courses provided at this prison. However, to break one's cycle of offending, more is needed – that is, making social changes, such as access to suitable housing and enabling individuals to meet certain economic necessities which protect them from criminal propensities. Rehabilitation programs often do not focus on the specific strains which are behind an individual's motivation to engage in crime. The IOPEP has taught me to reflect on this, something I would not have been able to do had I not participated in the program. I could not be as reflective about broader criminal justice issues, which is something I can use to reflect on my own offending.

During the COVID-19 pandemic, the Australian court system was overwhelmed, which resulted in a sudden increase in the unsentenced population. Due to strict gathering restrictions and social distancing guidelines, people were not able to attend court, which increased the backlog of cases remaining unheard and unresolved. Trials usually took about one to two years to be heard pre-COVID, but now it takes about anywhere from three to five years for a case to be scheduled for a hearing. I am currently on remand as I have not been yet found guilty of a crime. I feel very depressed when I think about this. I did not think it would be this easy to lock someone up while they wait for their trial date and are not yet found guilty of offending.

As part of my group assignment, we analyzed Singapore's corrections system. In Singapore, the Prison Service provides prisoners with only a straw mat and a blanket with no pillows. No drinking water is available outside of mealtimes. Prisoners are not allowed television or radio, and even pens and papers are banned. After hearing about these inhumane rules, I felt comparatively privileged and lucky to experience prison in Australia. With that said, there are many things that we can learn from Singapore. Singapore's reoffending rate 20 years ago was similar to Australia today, but has since dropped by half, while ours has remained the same. Singapore's prison service focused on rehabilitation by creating community awareness so that ex-prisoners get a chance to live normal lives in society without the burden of their criminal record. I think Australia has a lot to learn from Singapore in this respect. Singapore also has employment orientations, and 97 percent of prisoners find employment post-release. If people are working, they have a stable source of income and will, therefore, be less likely to participate in criminal activities.

Importantly, when the outside students first attended Ravenhall, they reminded me of myself before my incarceration. They assumed that the prison was an awful place full of dangerous and violent people. Throughout the IOPEP, they learned the truth — meeting the inside students 'humanized' prisoners and the prison experience for them. I hope that when they graduate and become professionals in their own right, they remember the plight and experiences of the inside students. Moreover, I hope that they treat the person before them like they treated us – with kindness. This program has been one of the most life-changing things I have ever done. When I go back to China, I want to make this type of change to the systems there – and I believe I can do it. Lastly, this program has given me confidence and inspired me to pursue university education.

In conclusion, the IOPEP has been an enlightening experience for me. It has allowed me to think about my imprisonment from an entirely different perspective. First, I have learned to critically analyze all aspects of the CJS and appreciate the complexities inherent in it. For example, every time I watch the news now and victims of crime are pushing for stricter sentencing laws, which often results in the government legislating mandatory sentencing laws, I understand why this occurs even though I may disagree with the government's decision. My learnings regarding policing, courts, and corrections have also allowed me to see my experience as potentially useful for the future improvement of the criminal justice system.

DISCUSSION

Despite the modified delivery of the IOPEP due to the COVID-19 pandemic, it is clear in Haozhou Sun's submitted reflection that many of its aims were still met. Most notably, the way in which IOPEP encourages inside students to interrogate their preconceived ideas about their criminal justice interaction. Further, IOPEP provided inside students with a purpose and a goal in what is frequently reflected as being "dead" or "wasted time" for those who are incarcerated. That is, the time in prison is referred to or experienced by many as a temporary "freeze on their life".

Another important outcome, not previously documented by Martinovic and colleagues (2018), which perhaps warrants further investigation, is the ability for inside students to view their circumstances of incarceration and experiences of disadvantage through a justice lens and scope. There are also strong reflexive themes which emanate from the reflection of Haozhou Sun, not merely describing the direness of his plight whilst incarcerated but composing it with the view to interrogate the way in which COVID-19 has brought about further injustices. Indeed, it is beyond the scope of this paper to further examine specifically the drivers of this thought, but it may be appropriate to speculate here that giving students a worldview of criminal justice systems gives inside students a yardstick to compare and contrast their experiences against the experience of others in different parts of the world. Despite Haozhou Sun conceding that although the Australian system provides material resources to lessen the physical deprivation experienced by others, for example in Singapore, there are still symbolic and tangible instruments which position incarcerated people in Australia as being subjugated. There is also further potential here to examine the way in which subordination whilst incarcerated is relative; that although being imprisoned in Singapore is unfavourable in the opinion of Haozhou Sun, he is critical of the Singaporean system as being an outlier and not the ideal, referring his circumstance back into the accepted standards of the broader Australian social landscape.

It can also be seen in Haozhou Sun's reflection that through his participation in the IOPEP, he has been able to critically reflect and thus challenge the stereotypes embedded in society, specifically identity constructions of how the "offender" is portrayed by broader society and mainstream discourse. The way in which he speaks of the injustice of the situation, describing his prolonged period on remand, is an example of dialogue which challenges current criminal justice policies. Whilst he is still incarcerated, there is real potential for Haozhou Sun to act on his reflections, and echo the results of other IOPEP evaluations (e.g. King et al., 2019).

A final theme that has been illuminated by Haozhou Sun is his reflection on the IOPEP forging an egalitarian learning community. This outcome has been well documented by evaluators of the IOPEP, most notably by Martinovic and colleagues (2018), along with King and colleagues (2019). A great example of this is the inquisitive nature of outside students in trying to understand the experience of incarceration through dialogue and conversation. Indeed, this type of learning experience can also be understood as being based on Freirean dialogic principles whereby learning is achieved through dialogue and a mutual appreciation of stakeholders within dialogue as knowledge-bearers. The philosophy of IOPEP is built on dialogic principles, taking away formal and traditional methods of pedagogy, and substituting it with experience and applied knowledge (Martinovic and Liddell, 2020; Antojado et al., 2023).

CONCLUSION

Haozhou Sun's reflection shows that although the delivery of IOPEP was modified to coincide with relevant pandemic regulations, it still allowed students to reflect on their experience as part of the wider, global criminal justice domain. The IOPEP has allowed Sun to be encouraged to pursue other ambitions within the correctional education space upon completion of the program. Most importantly, it has empowered Sun to become a part of criminal justice discourse, using his lived experience as a focal-point for future advocacy and insight. Although the pandemic did not provide Sun the same interaction with inside/outside students prior to the onset of the COVID-19 pandemic, an emergent theme in his reflection highlights the power of IOPEP to give meaning and purpose to those incarcerated whilst subject to the harsh prison conditions during this period.

REFERENCES

Allred, Sarah, Lana Harrison and Daniel O'Connell (2013) "Self-Efficacy: An Important Aspect of Prison-Based Learning", *The Prison Journal*, 93(2): 211-233.

Antojado, Dwayne (2022) "The Sociological Imagination: Reflections of a Prisoner in Australia", *European Journal of Behavioral Sciences*, 5(4): 21-30.

Antojado, Dwayne, Marietta Martinovic, Tarmi A'Vard, Grace Stringer and Chelsea Barnes (2023) "Inside Out and Think Tank Participation in Australia: Can Engaging with Lived Experience of Incarceration Promote Desistance?", *Journal of Advanced Research in Social Sciences*, 6(3): 76-84.

Butin, Dan (2013) "The Walls We Build and Break Apart: IOPEP as Transformational Pedagogy", in Simone Weil Davis and Barbara Sherr Roswell (eds.), *Turning Teaching Inside Out: A Pedagogy of Transformation*, New York: Palgrave, pp. ix-xii.

Conti, Norman, Linda Morrison and Katherine Pantaleo (2013) "All the Wiser: Dialogic Space, Destigmatization, and Teacher-Activist Recruitment", *The Prison Journal*, 93(2): 163-188.

Hilinski-Rosick, Carly and Alicia Blackmer (2014) "An Exploratory Examination of the Impact of the Inside-Out Prison Exchange Program", *Journal of Criminal Justice Education*, 25(3): 386-397.

Hyatt, Susan B. (2009) "Creating Social Change by Teaching Behind Bars: The Inside-Out Prison Exchange Program", *Anthropology News*, 50(1): 24-28.

Inside-Out Centre (2022) "World Reach Graph and Statistics". Retrieved from: https://www.insideoutcenter.org/about-IOPEP.html.

King, Hannah, Fiona Measham and Kate O'Brian (2019) "Building Bridges Across Diversity: Utilising the Inside-Out Prison Exchange Programme to Promote an Egalitarian Higher Education Community within Three English Prisons", *International Journal of Bias, Identity and Diversity in Education*, 4(1): 66-81.

Long, Daniel and Marvin Barnes (2016) *A Pilot Evaluation of the Inside-Out Prison Exchange Program in the Philadelphia*, Philadelphia: Research for Action.

Metzner, Jeffrey and Jamie Fellner (2010) "Solitary Confinement and Mental Illness in U.S. Prisons: A Challenge for Medical Ethics", *Journal of American Academy of Psychiatry Law*, 38(1): 104-108.

Martinovic, Marietta and Marg Liddell (2020) "Learning Behind Prison Bars: University Students and Prisoners' Experiences of Studying Together", in Darren Palmer (ed.), *Scholarship of Teaching and Learning in Criminology*, Berlin: Springer, pp. 37-58.

Martinovic, Marietta and Marg Liddell (2019) "Enhancing Diversity and Inclusion Through Students' Transformative Experiences in Prison", in Belinda Tynan, Tricia McLaughlin, Andrea Chester, Catherine Hall van den Elsen and Belinda Kennedy (eds.), *Transformations in Tertiary Education*, Singapore: Springer, pp. 11-26.

Martinovic, Marietta, Marg Liddell and Shane Douglas Muldoon (2018) "Changing Views and Perceptions: The Impact of the Australian Inside-Out Prison Exchange Program on Students", *Educational Research and Evaluation*, 24(6-7): 437-453.

O'Brien, Kate, Hannah King, Josie Phillips, Kath Dalton, and Phoenix (2021) "'Education as the Practice of Freedom?' Prison Education and the Pandemic", *Educational Review*, 74(3): 685-703.

Pollack, Shoshana (2019) "Transformative Praxis With Incarcerated Women: Collaboration, Leadership and Voice", *Affilia*, 35(3): 344–357.

Pollack, Shoshana and Christine Mayor (eds.) (2023) Special Issue: Walls to Bridges, *Journal of Prisoners on Prisons*, 32(1): 1-186.

Pompa, Lori (2002) "Service- Learning as Crucible: Reflection on Immersion, Context, Power, and Transformation", *Michigan Journal of Community Service Learning*, 9: 67-76.

Werts, Tyrone (2013) "Reflections on the Inside-Out Prison Exchange Program", *The Prison Journal*, 93(2): 135-138.

Wyant, Brian R. and Brian Lockwood (2018) "Transformative Learning, Higher Order Thinking, and the Inside-Out Prison Exchange Program", *Journal of Correctional Education*, 69(3): 49–67.

ABOUT THE AUTHORS

Dwayne Antojado is a researcher and academic with lived experience of the criminal justice system in Australia. He uses his lived experience to influence his research and advocacy work in academia, government, and the not-for-profit sector. He has led and worked on various projects embedding and amplifying lived experience perspectives in organizational practice, structure, and processes with organizations including the Australian Community Support Organisation, Jesuit Social Services, Vacro, and RMIT University's community-based and prison-based think tanks. Dwayne is currently an academic in the School of Social Sciences, Monash University, and La Trobe Law School, La Trobe University in Australia. He is also the Research Director for Humans of San Quentin, a story-telling project based in California, seeking to humanize the experiences of incarcerated people globally. His research interests include LGBTQI+ experiences in the justice system, lived experience criminology, education in prisons, and prison radio. He can be reached by email at dwayne.antojado@monash.edu or at the following address:

Dwayne Antojado
School of Social Sciences Menzies Building
20 Chancellors Walk
Monash University
Clayton VIC 3800, Australia

Haozhou Sun is a graduate of the Australian Inside-Out Prison Exchange Program run in collaboration with RMIT University's Criminology and Justice Discipline (School of Global, Urban and Social Studies), and the Victorian Department of Justice and Community Safety, Australia. He is a member of the prison-based Change on the Inside Think Tank based at Ravenhall Correctional Centre, Victoria, Australia.

Marietta Martinovic, PhD, is Associate Professor in Criminology and Justice Studies in the School of Global, Urban, and Social Studies, RMIT University, Melbourne, Australia. She started the first Australian Inside-Out Prison Exchange Program in Australia, and has established and is leading four prison-based and one community-based Think Tank. Her research interests include electronic monitoring, the Inside-Out Prison Exchange Program, and education in prisons. She can be reached by email at: marietta.martinovic@rmit.edu.au

An Ethnography of a Corrections Education Instructor: Critical Issues
Robert Elton

ABSTRACT

Incarceration comes with its own sets of difficulties. People are thrust into social situations that are antagonistic to typical life, such as defending against rape, fighting lengthy appeals, and living and working around often unfavourable people and conditions. Additional challenges are time and opportunity, resources, effective instruction, and psychological states of both students and instructors. This paper describes the universal challenges and subjective experiences as instructor for an adult basic education and general education program within the state operated prison context. The paper includes constructs that may help educators prepare and plan in such a dynamic and dangerous environment.

Key words: General education diploma; adult basic education; prison violence; corrections education; free-world

INTRODUCTION

Teaching and learning within the context of an adult correctional institution is much different from secondary and post-secondary environments in which we are used to in broader western society. For example, andragogy is a distinct field from pedagogy and the efforts of trying to instruct adults who have been incarcerated for crimes (and who will often remain so for years) eliminates much of the relatively immediate incentives for learning normally seen in free-world situations. Rather than transition from one grade to the next, or experience definite milestones such as graduations, the prisoner-student must figure out a way to achieve benchmarks without much accolade or celebration.

Generally, prisoners who have been assigned to an education program were found to need such a program via court order or general corrections case plan. For whatever reason, the incoming students have not finished high school nor completed a GED (general education diploma) prior to being imprisoned for crime and are assigned to be a student due to need. It has long been understood that earning an education can prevent recidivism (Ntombizanele, 2019), as well as contribute to financial stability and longer life expectancy (Luy, et al., 2019). Based on such policy foundations, we will continue to see corrections education programs up to the high school level at the very least.

METHODOLOGY

This paper is grounded in *participant-as-observer* methods as a form of qualitative approach (Jerolmack and Khan, 2018; Jorgensen, 2020). Ethnography has long been used and valued by researchers and is characterized "by in-depth observation of groups of individuals, being cognizant of the influences of historical and cultural contexts on social interactions" (Jones and Smith, 2017, p. 98). In fact, ethnographic research can "provide a deeper insight into a culture" (Shafik and Grant, 2011, p. 378). Ethnography has been found useful in a variety of contexts, such as anthropology, sociology, and even corrections (Thomas, 2014; Helfgott, 2018).

ANALYSIS

The instructional and learning issues within adult basic education and general education diploma contexts in prisons are unique and numerous. The primary issues are safety related and the secondary concerns are logistics, and actual learning. This is not so different facially from free-world experience, however, the environment and culture within which learning and instruction must occur is, in this writer's opinion, different, as discussed below.

Imprisoned adult learners, for example, are thrust into a living structure that is most foreign to human experience. They are further being mandated to participate and complete adult basic education and/or the GED after having previously failed the endeavour in the free-world. Research indicates that those people without any high school level diploma totals roughly "75 percent of America's state prison inmates" (Amos, 2010, n.p.). Three-out-of-every-four people imprisoned require a GED, either by court order as part of their sentence, or via a corrections plan. Conversely, less than one-in-three (27 percent) actually obtain the GED while imprisoned, according to Couloute (2018). The reality of this data did not begin to provide insight as to why. Though not exhaustive, this paper offers to fill the void in the data by offering a list of following prison conditions that were barriers to educational success that were either known or encountered by the author throughout his years as an instructor.

Subculture of Exploitation and Peer Pressure

Within prisons there are gangs, drug dealing, and other subversive endeavours such as beer-making, tattooing, and other antisocial forms of diversion. Self-improvement via educational attainment is a minor concern and some prisoners were very susceptible to how they might be viewed by other prisoners for attending classes. It is possible that some viewed all of these distractions as nearly insurmountable and acted in conformance to the attitudes of the general population as an easier lifestyle. These subversive endeavours are barriers in that they are ever-present and exist even after the diploma. These behaviours operate to increase absenteeism, diminish the opportunity to acquire and use newfound knowledge, which is to consequently reject a means to expand upon it.

Tackling these issues from an institutional standpoint is difficult at best. A sole instructor or culture of instruction is also at a disadvantage. This is especially true given the vast sizes of most prisons and that, in addition to distributive and logistical service issues, they are somewhat understaffed and staff are often not ambitious enough to undertake eradication of these issues.

Mental Health

While data in this area is conflicting, it nevertheless highlights another fundamental problem in corrections – there is an overrepresentation of mental health sufferers who make up around half of any state prison population. One study from the state of Virginia provided that 15 percent of its state prisoners suffer from severe mental illness (Torrey et al., 2014), whereas a Bureau of Justice Statistics report indicated as high as 49 percent suffer from a mental health disorder (BJS, 2006; also see Wainwright and Dawson, 2022). Finally, while addiction is an aspect of the mental health or medical sector, there was minimal interaction with these types of prisoners. This is particularly so because drug habits are unsustainable due to cost and supply within a prison setting. There may have been comorbidity with mental health issues and addiction, but mostly limited attention span and/ or hyperactivity were both prevalent in the classroom and in the one-on-one tutoring context. One had to strain for a miraculous level of creativity and affect to impart the nuances of the Pythagorean Theorem and the order of operations to encourage focus in this demographic.

Violence and Lockdowns

Violence in prisons is another reality that detracts from concentration on one's education. To obtain and retain knowledge, one needs persistent interaction with the material and time for the endeavour. Lockdowns are prevalent due to violence, as are shakedowns for drugs and other contraband, and rare situations such as was experienced through the COVID-19 pandemic. Prior to the vaccine rollout, there was no education program, nor mass congregation of prisoners for eating, nor religious services. These are uncontrollable situations.

Dated Resources in the Internet Age

Quasi-related to attention span is that students are limited to dated materials. Even those students with access to computers lack sufficient computer skills. Typing and navigating programs are typical skills that are rare in the prison context. Even having access to a computer is an issue, largely due to perceived security interests. In the internet age, knowledge is easier to locate and access than in any time in history, yet prisoners are kept from this revolution. Resources taken for granted by free-world people such as Google search, Google Scholar, YouTube, and other online databases are absent. These sites would make teaching and learning much easier.

CONCLUSION

Instruction in the state prison context is fraught with problems which serve to diminish the capacity and ability for educational attainment. Environmental factors to the student such as violence, drugs, hustling, and other antisocial distractions are more attractive activities than learning algebra and developing language comprehension. This is further complicated by administrative functions such as lockdowns (and pandemics) and even instructor inadequacy.

Students also sometimes have internal challenges such as mental health issues, self-esteem, or perhaps even learning disabilities which have not been addressed. Drug addiction may be co-morbid to personality disorders or mental health issues but were not seen to determine or influence educational success in terms of completion of the GED.

Instructors considering a career in corrections education would benefit from learning about the occupation from those who practice or have had experience in prison education context. In this way, one can discern employment goodness-of-fit before applying. If one is encouraged to attempt this occupation, it has to be with a full understanding that instructing in the context of a prison setting may demand the best of oneself and, when one least expects it, perhaps make a difference in the lives of others.

REFERENCES

Amos, Jason (2010) "New PEW report: Young black men without a high school diploma are more likely to be found in a cell than in the workplace", *Alliance for Excellent Education* – October 6. Retrieved from: https://all4ed.org/new-pew-report-young-black-men-without-a-high-school-diploma-are-more-likely-to-be-found-in-a-cell-than-in-the-workplace/

Couloute, Lucius (2018) "Getting back on course: Educational exclusion and attainment among formerly incarcerated people", *Prison Policy Initiative* – October. Retrieved from: https://www.prisonpolicy.org/reports/education.html

Dharamsi, Shafikk and Grant Charles (2011) "Ethnography: Traditional and Criticalist Conceptions of a Qualitative Research Method", *Canadian Family Physician*, 57(3): 378-379.

James, Doris and Lauren Glaze (2006) *Mental Health Problems of Prison and Jail Inmates* – September, Washington: Bureau of Justice Statistics.

Jerolmack, Colin and Shamus Khan (2018) *Approaches to Ethnography: Analysis and Representation in Participant Observation*, Oxford: Oxford University Press.

Jones, Janice and Joanna Smith (2017) "Ethnography: Challenges and Opportunities", *Evidence Based Nursing*, 20(4): 98-100.

Jorgensen, Danny (2020) *Principles, Approaches and Issues in Participant Observation*, London: Routledge.

Helfgott, Jacqueline B. (2018) "Searching for Glimmers of Ethnography in Jailhouse Criminology", in Stephen Rice and Michael Maltz (eds.), *Doing Ethnography in Criminology*, Cham: Springer, pp. 203-222.

Luy, Marc, Marina Zannella, Christian Wegner-Siegmundt, Yuka Minagawa, Wolfgang Lutz and Graziella Caselli (2019) "The Impact of Increasing Education Levels on Rising Life Expectancy: A Decomposition Analysis for Italy, Denmark, and the USA", *Genus*, 75(1): 11.

Treatment Advocacy Center (2016) Serious Mental Illness Prevalence in Jails and Prisons – September. Retrieved from: https://www.treatmentadvocacycenter.org/evidence-and-research/learn-more-about/3695

Ugelvik, Thomas (2014) "Prison Ethnography as Lived Experience: Notes from the Diaries of a Beginner Let Loose in Oslo Prison", *Qualitative Inquiry*, 20(4): 471-480.

Vandala, Ntombizanele Gloria (2019) "The Transformative Effect of Correctional Education: A Global Perspective", *Cogent Social Sciences*, 5(1).

Wainwright, Verity and Alice Dawson (2022) "The Prevalence of Comorbid Substance Use Disorders and Serious Mental Illnesses in Prisons", *The Lancet Public Health*, 7(6): e492-e493.

ABOUT THE AUTHOR

Robert Elton, ThD, MSc, BA, AAS, AA is the author of *Grey Areas: Interdisciplinary Concepts and the Crafters of Social Science.* He is pursuing a second doctorate in Criminal Justice at Northcentral University and has taught several courses as a volunteer while imprisoned including adult basic education.

The Second Coming (Out)
Matthew Feeney

During my first week in prison, my name was called over the P.A. for a visit and I was stunned when the entire cell block started chanting, "HO-MO! HO-MO! HO-MO!" It was just like those classic prison movies right before a riot breaks out: loud, scary, and intimidating as hell. Shaken, I went to my visit and shared the experience with my parents. I told them I did not know how I had been outed as a gay man to the entire cell block, and I remember naively stating my profound relief that "at least they don't know I'm a sex offender". Two hours later, I returned to my cell block only to learn everyone had actually been chanting "CHO-MO" — prison slang for a child molester.[1] Thus, began my six-year prison sentence. Remarkably, I survived and served my entire prison sentence, the maximum allowed by law.

I was then civilly committed. Civil commitment still exists in 20 states and consists of additional time served in a prison-like facility for the exact same crimes for which one served their prison time.[2] I am now serving a new "indeterminate" (de facto life) sentence in a state mental asylum, known as the Minnesota Sex Offender Program (MSOP), which Federal Judge Donovan Frank has called "draconic". Civil commitment in general, and within the MSOP specifically, is wrought with Civil Rights issues. On 1 July 2022, the United States Department of Justice (DOJ) filed an Amicus Curiae brief supporting the clients at MSOP and demanding immediate changes and reforms.[3] Even England's Highest Court of Justice has specifically ruled Minnesota's civil commitment law to be "a flagrant denial of... rights enshrined under Article 5.1" of the European Convention on Human Rights (ECHR).[4]

I am attracted to males and have been all my life. Back when I was growing up, being homosexual was not only socially unacceptable, but it was also actually illegal and considered a diagnosable mental illness. This abhorrence towards same-sex attractions was reinforced growing up in a Catholic family, which included my attending a Catholic High School followed by a Catholic College. Living under the severe homophobia of the Roman Catholic church during these formative years taught me that my sexual attraction towards my male classmates meant I was "intrinsically flawed". I was encouraged to "love the sinner but hate the sin". It was bad enough to hear masturbation was morally wrong, but as a normal teenager with a healthy imagination, I was mortified to learn even thinking sexual thoughts was apparently just as sinful as committing the act itself. I felt as though I was screwed, so I buried all my secret attractions and fought like hell to hide and deny my homosexuality. I tried dating females in college and even explored becoming a priest as a valid, if not noble, explanation as to why I was still single and a virgin. I was not happy or healthy.

The American Psychiatric Association eventually dropped homosexuality as a diagnosable mental disorder, but I never got the memo. I struggled with loving myself and never got over the shame I was forced to carry about my homosexuality. Even after eventually coming out of the closet, I was a damaged man with very low self-esteem and embarrassed by my lack of sexual experience. Eventually, I tried to find acceptance with males younger than myself, including teenagers.

I fully admit I screwed up. I broke the law. I betrayed my friends and family, while causing inexorable harm to innocent people. I tried guilty "straight up" (without any plea agreement) and I gladly served the maximum sentence allowable under Minnesota state law. While incarcerated in the Minnesota Department of Corrections, I underwent three years of intensive sex offender therapy run by MSOP. Homophobia ran rampant in this program, as evidenced by the fact when gay men were given polygraphs, they were asked if they have sexually acted out, while straight prisoners were asked about selling Ramen noodles. I had ample opportunities to have consensual sexual activity with attractive prisoners, some who humorously self-identified as "gay for the stay, but straight at the gate", but I chose not to. Knowing the possibility of civil commitment was looming over my head, I knew that any sexual activity while in prison would be used against me during my civil commitment trial as evidence of me not being cured, and that I was unable to control my deviant sexual desires even when under intense supervision.

As my six-year prison sentence was nearing completion, I was informed that the State of Minnesota was pursuing civil commitment for me. Instead of releasing me, they scheduled me for civil court trial. They used the same facts and criminal history that precipitated my original prison sentence to now claim that I had a mental disorder and needed to be locked up for the rest of my life in a secure mental hospital. Several of the homophobic actuarial tools used to assess potential targets for civil commitment raise your risk score if you provide an affirmative answer to "has at least one male victim". Partly due to such biased "tools", homosexuals are vastly overrepresented in the civil commitment population, with a recent survey showing well over 60 percent of MSOP clients identifying as LGBTQ+. My only current mental health diagnosis is that I am sexually attracted to other males, including post-pubescent (late teenage) males.

Of course, the MSOP civil commitment "treatment" program is actually a cruel joke used to provide the required legality for an otherwise unconstitutional civil commitment program. Like the Catholic Church, MSOP promotes total abstinence and the program specifically prohibits any healthy sexual activity of any kind between clients, some who have been civilly committed for over 30 years. Despite the courts determining we are apparently unable to control our deviant sexual behaviour, MSOP forces me to live, sleep, and defecate in the same private room as another gay man. I would love to see a heterosexual male DOC prisoner forced to live for years in the same bedroom with an attractive woman without becoming physical. However, anyone caught violating MSOP's policies is locked up in segregation, written up with multiple BERs ("Behavioural Expectation Reports"), and punished with room restrictions, loss of privileges, and having to do additional "treatment assignments" connecting their current "acting out" to their original offending behaviour. Since I have been locked up, same-sex marriage has become legal in Minnesota. While MSOP policy has to now officially allow two male clients to get legally married, the married couple is still subject to the same "no touch" restrictions – they are moved to separate living units and not allowed any physical contact or display of affection.

Ironically, my Special Release Board (SRB) assessor noted that, "It appears Mr. Feeney has had one romantic relationship throughout his life and desires to be in a romantic relationship in the future... It will be important for Mr. Feeney to explore what contributes to a healthy relationship and strengthen his ability to communicate his thoughts and feelings with a partner, taking appropriate steps to get his sexual and emotional needs met". A second SRB assessor noted, "Mr. Feeney's capacity for relationship stability will remain a risk factor for him until he has resided with a romantic partner in a stable relationship in the community for two years". It is frustrating to be told I will not be released until I can reduce my risk by exploring healthy adult sexuality, but then I am forced to live in a place in which that is an impossibility.

It is ominously comfortable for this recovering Catholic to once again be living in such a homophobic environment where I am being constantly watched, as well as reminded how any and all sexual activity is bad and needs to be kept as a dirty little secret because we will get punished if we are caught. No wonder no one ever completes this "treatment" program when healthy, consensual same-sex sexual activity is not only punished, but used against us in court as further evidence of our deviancy and need for further confinement. This program makes the old fashioned "ex-gay conversion therapy" seem like summer camp.

So here I am, an openly gay man, spending the rest of my life in a mental hospital, which is pretending to provide "treatment" for a homosexual, regardless of that fact that I have already served my entire prison sentence for having inappropriate sexual relations. I am told that, in order to get released, I need to work on cultivating healthy sexuality, but I am forced to live inches away from another gay man, while being simultaneously prohibited from engaging in any consensual age-appropriate same-sex relationships. Furthermore, this "treatment" is costing taxpayers $404.00 a day for the rest of my life. It is time to end the atrocity.

ENDNOTES

[1] The exact terminology seems to vary by region. In Massachusetts, the term is "Ripper" (pronounced Rippa) or "Skinner" (pronounced Skinna).

[2] According to the Association of Treatment of Sexual Abusers' website (www.atsa. com), as of 2015, the 21 states with civil commitment laws were Arizona, California, Florida, Illinois, Iowa, Kansas, Massachusetts, Minnesota, Missouri, Nebraska, New Hampshire, New Jersey, New York, North Dakota, Pennsylvania, South Carolina, Texas, Virginia, Washington, Wisconsin, and the District of Columbia. Pennsylvania's law is unique in that it applies only to youth adjudicated for a sexual offense who are "aging out" of the juvenile justice system.

[3] Federal District Court File No. 0:11-cv-03659.

[4] Sullivan v The Government of the United States of America (Case No: C0/1672/2011).

ABOUT THE AUTHOR

Matthew Feeney is currently imprisoned. For further information on the initiatives he is involved in, join the Facebook group "End MSOP" and check out national organizations fighting against civil commitment such as CURE-SORT.arg, NARSOL, and aJustFuture.org. He can be reached at the following address:

Matthew Feeney
1111 Highway 73
Moose Lake, MN 55767
USA

Gender Not Fit for Prisons:
On The Incompatibility of Gender
as a Means to Segregate Prisoners
Dwayne Antojado

ABSTRACT

Prisons worldwide, including in Australia, are segregated based on biological sex. On the other hand, feminist scholarship challenges gender within the binary of man and woman, arguing instead that individuals undergo the process of "becoming" and are not merely born. In this space, tensions exist for transgender individuals interacting with prisons. Although many policy initiatives are being established by correctional authorities world-wide, these innovations are often criticized for failing to translate into reality. It is argued here that prisons must reimagine the way they categorize individuals based on binary conceptions of gender. Instead, they must view gender through the optics of transgenderism, where it is conceived as something fluid, changing, and mutable.

INTRODUCTION

Prisons worldwide, including in Australia, are segregated based on biological sex (Rodgers et al., 2017). On the other hand, feminist scholarship challenges gender within the binary of man and woman, arguing instead that individuals undergo the process of becoming and are not merely born (de Beauvoir, 1949). In this space, serious tensions exist for transgender individuals interacting with social institutions (including prisons), rendering transgenderism incoherent with social gender constructions. For transgender individuals, this tension is lived and contributes to their overall experience of structural sex and gender discrimination. It is argued here that prisons and other social institutions must implement policies geared towards bettering the conditions and interactions of transgender individuals with prisons by admitting transgender prisoners based on gender and not biological sex.

Further, traditional constructions of gender that fit within the dualism of man or woman are incoherent with gender constructions under the optics of transgenderism. Therefore, policy initiatives and innovations must have regard for the fluidity of sex and gender, and be careful not to perpetuate structural discrimination through traditionalist perspectives.

Moreover, this paper centralizes the work of Singer (2013) in interrogating the incongruity of transgenderism within binary schemas, particularly within broader social institutions.

INCONGRUITY OF TRANSGENDERISM

"Classificatory schemas that ascribed gender attribution, enforce gender socialization, and assign sex at birth is usually dimorphic: male/female" (Singer, 2013, p. 2). As a result, these schemas make bodies socially useful, culturally legible, and productive under different regimes of power (Singer, 2013). The inability for transgenderism to be articulated within these understandings, and the incongruity between bodies, identities, assigned gender, and gender expression (Singer, 2013), explicates the institutional betrayal of social life, government, and its processes in actively marginalizing transgender people through discriminative, exclusive, and phobic social structures. Of these, prison is a salient example, causing deleterious effects for transgender people (Maycock, 2020). Incorporating academic understandings gained through transgender studies into interrogative discussions of structural transphobia, including the experiences of transgender people as violators of sex and gender norms (Singer, 2013), is key to enriching public policy initiatives geared towards mitigating the effects of how gender is socially constructed. Moreover, it can inform policy initiatives to see transgenderism as a progressive and enriching tool forwarding the feminist project.

SEX, GENDER AND TRANSGENDERISM

Sex and gender theorists explain the attainment of gender through processes that include socialisation (Hoominfar, 2021) and performativity (Butler, 2006). An example is the gendering of colour (Wikberg, 2013), articulated thorough social constructs which assign colour to gender. For example, blue is often associated with the male gender, whereas pink is associated with the female gender (socialisation). As these gendered associations of colour are embedded into the child's psyche, it is performed and expressed socially (performativity) as an endeavour to conform to specific and prescribed gender dispositions, including personality traits and behaviours indicative of the broader social belief that masculinity is prescribed for men and femininity for women (Richardson, 2015). Furthermore, during the nineteenth century and early in the twentieth century, scientific theories dominated discourses of gender (Richardson, 2015). These theories reflected "biological" and "natural" explanations of human behavior, positing that these "sex differences" produced discernible psychological and behavioural dispositions in both males and females (Richardson, 2015).

From the outset, biological and naturalist explanations, and the gendering of particular objects, simplified social perceptions of man and woman into dichotomous and inflexible categories, in which transgenderism is incongruent. For example, clothing products for male customers are marketed using cisgender male models. Likewise, products for female consumers are marketed utilizing cisgender female models, inferring cisgenderism as being desired and socially prescribed, similar to Martino's (1999) notion of "desirable masculinities" (p. 243). In this realm, sex is inextricably intertwined with gender and is not perceived as being two separate social constructions that do not collude. These cumulative societal explanations and perceptions of sex and gender account for transgenderism, contributing to the construction of transphobia. That is, "the fear, intolerance, or hatred of people who are, or who perceive to be transgender" (Gainsburg, 2020). However, as Spade (2011, as cited in Singer, 2013) argues, transphobia does not sufficiently describe the state administrative practices that oppress transgender people, but rather an "intersectional analysis of the classed and racialized criminalization of gender nonconforming lives" (p. 3) is better equipped to understanding the structural harms faced by transgender people. In other words, examining transphobia within a specific institutional context should not be discussed in isolation, but rather factors contributing to the social structures that perpetuate transphobia must be interrogated through an intersectional lens.

STRUCTURAL TRANSPHOBIA IN PRISONS

Governmental institutions do not openly and overtly commit transphobia within prisons, but rather it is employed through structural policies, reflecting, reinforcing, and reinscribing the conceptual understanding of sex and gender within broader society. Feinberg (1992, as cited in Singer, 2013) infers the cause of transphobia to be an effect of the "[violations of] socially, culturally, and state-enforced boundaries of sex and gender" (p. 1). Further, these boundaries could be explained as a residue of Christian values, indoctrinated into laws and institutions due to colonization. For example, Hall and colleagues (2010) found in a study of harassment that religious beliefs moderated the effects of harassment. The penal estate in Australia is dichotomized based on biological sex assigned at birth – men and women are not intermingled with each other (Rodgers et al., 2017). The problem that transgenderism poses to the penal estate is that it does not fit into the categorical mechanisms employed to achieve social order and cohesion – transgenderism violates these gender norms (Singer, 2013). Transgender individuals identify their gender as being different to that of their sex (ibid). The policy guiding the segregation of prisons (within the Victorian [Australia] context) dictates that a person's initial custody placement, so as to coincide with prescribed gender norms, must be based on sex and not gender (e.g., Corrections Act 1986 [Vic]; Corrections Victoria, Department of Justice and Community Safety, 2021).

There are, of course, practical explanations that substantiate these practices. For example, the Corrections Regulation 2019 (Victoria) stipulates the procedure of "strip searches" (cl. 86) as a combatant against the trafficking of illegal substances to prisons from the general community. This is, of course, important as research infers that a significant number of prisoners held in custody are charged or have been found guilty of a drug-related crime (Duke, 2003). It is common practice for strip searches to be facilitated by a custodial officer of the same biological sex (Corrections Regulations 2019, cl. 82(2G)). As the transgender community is not a homogenous group (Harris, 2017), not all of its members have undergone medical intervention. Therefore, there may be differences between sex and gender. For example, some transgender women may still have or consciously choose to have their natural/biological defining features intact. However, they may have undergone breast augmentation. In this instance, how would the prison facilitate strip searches consistent with the laws of the State? Perhaps, a female officer could inspect the top half of the person's body, for they resemble a female's biological anatomy. Therefore, perhaps a male officer inspects the bottom half under the same rationale. Suppose prisons adopt this practice of officers inspecting part of a transgender person's body in isolation, indicative of their biological sexual features. Are prisons not merely perpetuating, condoning, and exacerbating transphobia for these practices signify social rejection and ignorance against transgenderism? If a person identifies as a woman, then that person should be stripped-searched based on how they identify, irrespective of their biological sex.

Moreover, these practices have individual psychological harms on transgender individuals. A helpful framework to understand these various harms is Meyer's (2003) Minority Stress Theory (MST). According to Meyer (2003), minority stress is the "excess stress to which individuals from stigmatized social categories are exposed to as a result of their social, often minority, position" (p. 675). Meyer (2003) originally developed MST as a way to account for the effects of minority stress on the mental health of specific sexual minority groups, typically, lesbian, gay, and bisexual (LGB) individuals. Since then, tokenistic incorporation of transgender individuals has been included in the conceptual framework of MST. Interestingly, Clarke and colleagues (2010) found that the stressors experienced by transgender individuals do not necessarily align with those experienced by their LGB counterparts. Consequently, Testa and colleagues (2015) developed an extension of MST referred to as Gender Minority Stress Theory (GMST), which considers the specific stressors transgender individuals experience. GMST asserts that minority stress experienced by transgender individuals are not only different but often more deleterious. A prevalent cause of this is cisnormativity. That is, the assumption that it is "normal" for an individual's gender identity to align with its biological or physical features assigned at birth. Correctional policy, such as the process of strip-searching of transgender individuals exampled above, indicate the prevalence of cisnormativity within the corrections space. GMST forwards the idea that cisnormativity elevates the likelihood of mental health problems experienced by transgender individuals by exposing them to trauma and spaces which reflect their secondary and subordinated social position. Therefore, not only does the strip search process exampled above perpetuate structural transphobia, but it potentially adds more harm by way of trauma, anxiety, and distress to transgender individuals. Research shows that trauma, anxiety, and distress all elevate an individual's propensity to re-offend (Smith and Trimboli, 2010), further exacerbating the position of transgender and gender diverse cohorts within the criminal justice space.

So far, this essay has interrogated the work of sex and gender as a cultural artefact that inadvertently subordinates transgender people through norming social structures due to their deviance from expected gender norms. The work of Maycock (2020) highlights the pains of imprisonment (as adapted from

Sykes, 1958) transgender people undergo individually whilst in custody. That is, the deprivations or frustrations of prison life experienced by transgender people resultant of these social structures (Maycock, 2020). Some of the difficulties faced by transgender people in prisons include "issues relating to transitioning within custody, being housed in prison wings of gender assigned at birth, and not lived gender, misgendering, misnaming, and experiences of transphobia and stigma perpetrated by other people in custody and by prison staff" (ibid, p. 2). Maycock argues that these "pains not only illuminate aspects of life in custody… but more widely illuminate the challenges associated with the growing diversity of gender performance being made to fit within largely binary prison systems" (ibid, p. 8). Maycock's (2020) research involved 13 transgender participants incarcerated in the Scottish correctional space, 11 of whom are transgender women and the remainder transgender men. The plight of transgender people in the context of prisons is harmful to those undergoing the incarceration experience and to the community in which the prison serves as a deterrent mechanism, desisting crime. During their time in prison, transgender people are significantly more likely to experience problems than other prison populations, including placement within the prison establishment based on anatomy and not gender performance, victimization, treatment, and healthcare provisions (Gorden et al., 2017). Most of the pains recounted by research participants resonate with those experienced by cisgender prisoners. However, several particular transgender-specific pains, which can be posited as residual outcomes of structural gender norms, emerged within the research findings. These included: the pains of being in the hall and in the wrong clothes, the pains of transitioning in custody, and the pains of isolation.

However, an important point of consideration is that despite potential developments in transgender policy, the plight of transgender people in prison will always be of concern. Prisons and the mechanisms that support the commission of prisons are itself producers of transgender inequalities, best captured by Stanley and colleagues (2012) who note: "the only prison that would be responsive to gender is one that ceases to exist" (p. 122). Stanley and colleagues argue that all innovations that aim to better the experiences of gay and transgender people are centered around the notion that we need a system of incarceration in the first place. That intervention can be put into place to minimize the gendered harms experienced by gay and transgender communities. However, artefacts of the prison industry will always reproduce these harms. These can be manifestly observed through regulations and rules, which include gendered dress codes, gendered behavioural codes, and hierarchical systems. For example, even if transgender and gender diverse individuals were to be housed in a location reflective of their lived gender, they must still adhere to the gendered norms within that institution. As argued above, transgenderism is fluid and cannot sufficiently captured through binary conceptions. However, whilst abolitionist perspectives concerning transgender experience bring to light important considerations, it is beyond the scope of this article to fully explore the plethora of insights researched within abolitionist scholarship.

DEVELOPMENTS IN PRISON POLICY

It is notable to mention that some advancements to the plight of transgender people are occurring, allowing for transgender incarcerated people to be held in custodial settings commensurate to their gender and not their biological sex assigned at birth (see Lamble, 2012). In the United Kingdom, transgender individuals who have attained a Gender Recognition Certificate (GRC) under the *Gender Recognition Act* (2004) can be detained at an institution that reflects their gender. Although the transgender community welcomes this initiative, Lamble (2012) elucidates critical practical implications that the GRC does not sufficiently mitigate in addressing the experiences of transgender people in prison. Despite transgender prisoners obtaining a GRC, prisons in the United Kingdom are still reluctant to classify them according to the gender indicated on the GRC citing that holding a transgender person in custody indicative of their identified gender poses a "security risk" (Lamble, 2012, p. 8) to the prison. Within this context, public policy has kept abreast with the scholarship of transgender studies. However, this policy initiative remains obsolete to its purported intention. A possible explanation of this practice is through an interrogation of reductionist and essentialist perceptions geared towards describing transgender people into one monolithic community. That is all transgender people, despite a proportion seeking medical intervention in an attempt to conform to prescribed gender norms, present in such a way that is still obfuscating and discombobulating for societal acceptance. As a residue of this rejection, it is assumed that all transgender people manifest their identities in a way that is discordant with the perceptions of the prison population, causing hostility. And yet, while there is cognizance of this, initiatives, intervention, and other transgender-specific projects are not undertaken by the penal estate – projects that could perhaps have the potential to quash assumptions associated with transgenderism that lead to their inability to participate in gender spaces reflective of theirs. In some ways, these experiences of structural transphobia documented by Lamble (2012) echoes Foucauldian perspectives on how prison is inherently oppressive, regardless of benevolent ideals (Jouet, 2021).

Within the Victorian (Australia) context, the 2.4.1 Commissioner's Requirement (CV, DJCS, 2021) published in March 2021 echoed the objectives of the GRC in the United Kingdom. However, like its predecessor, transgender prisoners' placement in prison is contingent on security and safety protocols. Clause 6.1 informs, "as a guiding principle, a person should be imprisoned in the prison of their gender rather than their sex assigned or assumed at birth" (ibid, p. 5). However, clause 6.5.1 of the same document states, "these decisions will be made with a view to ensuring the safety and welfare of the prisoner and other prisoners, as well as the security and good order of the prison" (ibid, p. 7). Currently, no study has evaluated the policies and procedures concerning this newly established strategy. However, if Corrections Victoria (CV) and the Department of Justice and Community Safety (DJCS) follows the steps of the GRC in the United Kingdom, it would undoubtedly be a worrying trajectory for transgender individuals. It would be helpful to analyze this policy in the future after it has been in place for some time to evaluate its efficacy and fidelity to guiding principles.

Another important note to consider in interrogating transgenderism in prisons is that "transgender does not only denote a specific type of identity and political collective; it also emphasizes transversal movement across boundaries of sex and gender relative to specific social structures and cultures" (Singer, 2013, pp. 1-2). Meaning that for transgender people, gender is not a dualism of male and female, but rather is a fluid notion that cannot be categorized. Therefore, structural policies aimed at alleviating transphobia through policy initiatives such as the implementation of the GRC and CR 2.4.1 must have regard to the fluidity of transgenderism (Singer, 2013). Cultural and social schemas of the dualism of male and female do not fit into the transgender lens of what gender is and the way it manifests. Ultimately, for policy initiatives such as the GRC and CR 2.4.1 to reach their potential utilitarian effect, it must encapsulate gender through the optics of transgenderism. Current structures of gender are limiting and have been shown to perpetuate imbalanced power relations that hinder the objectives of the feminist project (Ortner, 1974, as cited in Brown, 1981). The transgender optic of gender may be the missing ingredient of the feminist project towards equality.

LACK OF TRANSGENDER SPECIFIC INTERVENTIONS

It has been established that the role of prisons within the context of social life is to act as a deterrent from antisocial behaviours and attitudes which risk the order and cohesion of society (Apel and Nagin, 2015) through its various rehabilitative functions. As criminological research expanded and the academic scholarship realized the inefficiency of prisons, rehabilitation was soon introduced as one of the primary functions of the penal estate (Apel and Nagin, 2015). Thus, intervention and treatment were incorporated into the fabric of prison culture. Further, research elaborated the need for prisons to resemble therapeutic spaces (e.g. Bennet and Shuker, 2018; Williams and Winship, 2018) that encourage active participation in rehabilitation projects and reintegration initiatives, reducing the anxieties and difficulties inherent with leaving the prison experience. These projects were all established as a response, upholding and protecting the pillar of community safety as the ultimate objective of criminal justice, recognizing the difficulties prisoners face during and after prison.

Studies have illustrated the difficulties and challenges associated with being a transgender person in the community (e.g. Dernberger, 2017), suggesting the elevated problems transgender people experience after the prison spell compared to their cisgender counterparts. Intervention-specific projects geared towards rehabilitating transgender individuals, considering inimitable rehabilitation goals, including reducing the difficulties faced by transgender people in the community (Melendez and Pinto, 2007), are few and far between. The failure of prisons in establishing these initiatives reduces its efficacy within its purported community safety objective. The dearth of practical policy and attention reflects society's appetite, or lack thereof, in not accepting transgenderism as part of the gender norm, but also a reflection of its inability to see transgenderism as an enriching component of the feminist project.

RECOMMENDATIONS

Some practical and essential steps need to be enacted to reduce the experiences of discrimination and transphobia among transgender individuals. Firstly, due to the fluidity of gender within the transgender optics, it must be a long-term goal to segregate prisoners based on socialised gender. In the interim, transgender prisoners must be given a choice, at the first possible opportunity, on the location of their accommodation – whether in a male or female prison. For first time prisoners, their location may seem trivial as they will not know the difference in facilities between institutions for men and women. However, to reduce the elevated stress and anxiety experienced by transgender individuals, they should have the choice to decide. Additionally, the penal estate must not assess their suitability on whether or not they are "masculine enough" or "feminine enough" to fit in with the cohort of prisoners within that prison. Corrections must house transgender prisoners in establishments in which they are comfortable to foster a therapeutic and rehabilitative experience – one where transgender individuals willingly engage in clinical and non-clinical rehabilitation programs.

Secondly, alleviating the experiences of transphobia within the prison cannot be remedied in isolation. Projects that simultaneously address individuals' perceptions about sex and gender norms, transgender and gender diverse myths, and prisoner and prison staff culture, to name a few, are also significant in quashing cisnormative views and structures. For example, educational forums and programs may be organized by correctional institutions as a way to facilitate organic conversations about transgenderism, encouraging curiosity among members of staff and prisoners, and paving the way for social change. It would also be essential to amplify the voices of transgender and gender diverse prisoners to shed light on their experiences to enrich the corrections space in creating policy and protocols. Transgender individuals should have input in any policy initiative that directly relates to their carceral experience.

Thirdly, as with the social change project above, university curriculums need to be amended to include transgender-specific training. Higher education institutions produce future criminal justice practitioners, and yet anecdotal accounts indicate that most universities do not equip professionals with the skills to handle inimitable issues faced by transgender and gender diverse populations in the criminal justice arena. Early research points to the often complex and interrelated factors that lead transgender and gender diverse cohorts to take on criminally deviant behaviours, consequently leading to criminal justice interactions (e.g. Jumper, 2021). Providing useful training to criminal justice practitioners will enable them to more efficiently and adequately assist transgender individuals during and after their time in prison. The three recommendations explicated above are not exhaustive measures. Instead, they are first-step initiatives that require immediate implementation and attention by correctional and governmental institutions.

CONCLUSION

This paper has demonstrated the need to reorganize the segregation of prisons away from dichotomized, essentialist, and biological basis. Biology is not destiny. A woman's ability to reproduce does not in itself constitute her gender. The fluidity and mutability of sex and gender through the optics of transgenderism as a means to segregate social institutions, like prisons, provides a more holistic and complete template, which accounts for the miscellany of identities associated with the term transgender. Heteronormative constructions and assumptions on how bodies are defined and engaged with have clear implications for transgender individuals. Although recent developments in governmental and institutional policies have been enacted to ameliorate the experiences of transgender individuals, more work still needs to be done to synthesize policy with actual experienced outcomes. To this end, studies are needed, particularly evaluating current practices and policies such as CV, DJCS, 2021. It is then crucial for governmental bodies to utilize these studies to better equip the penal estate in dealing with transgender prisoners, ensuring that academic epistemologies are at the forefront of governmental policy.

Moreover, it is vital to establish transgender-specific innovations, recognizing the interrelated and complex problems transgender people face during and after the prison experience. By extension, it is insufficient for prisons to essentialize all prisoners, especially transgender and other gender diverse individuals, into one monolithic community. This has significant implications for its rehabilitative and deterrent utility within the broader criminal justice system. Allowing transgender individuals to be placed contingent on their lived gender would be an essential first step towards ameliorating structural transphobia.

Finally, the recommendations above need to have immediate effect. The harms faced by the transgender community in prison are pervasive and continued. However, these experiences of distress, invisibility, and transphobia lived by transgender people in prison can be alleviated, which requires society to look profoundly into how it functions, categorizes, discerns, and distinguishes people based on differences. It must reimagine the utility of sex and gender as a tool to categorize and sort in order for the potential of transgenderism to be realized, supporting the alleviation of transphobia not only in prisons but in the broader community.

ACKNOWLEDGEMENTS

Thank you to Dr. Josephine Browne of Griffith University (Australia), Dr. Marietta Martinovic and Scarlet Rosa of RMIT University (Australia), Dr. Greg Newbold of the University of Canterbury (New Zealand), and Adrien McCrory of the Australian Catholic University, for reading early drafts of this paper and providing insightful and useful suggestions.

REFERENCES

Apel, Robert and Daniel Nagin (2015) "Deterrent Effect of Police and Prisons", in James Wright (ed.), *International Encyclopedia of the Social & Behavioral Sciences*, Amsterdam: Elsevier, pp. 260-265.

Bennett, Jamie and Richard Shuker (2018) "Hope, Harmony and Humanity: Creating a Positive Social Climate in a Democratic Therapeutic Community Prison and the Implications for Penal Practice", *Journal of Criminal Psychology*, 8(1): 44-57.

Brown, Jordanova (1981) "Oppressive Dichotomies: The Nature/Culture Debate", in Cambridge Women's Studies Group (ed.), *Women in Society: Interdisciplinary Essays*, London: Virago, pp. 221-224.

Butler, Judith (2006) *Gender Trouble: Feminism and the Subversion of Identity*, London: Routledge.

Clarke, Victoria, Sonja Ellis, Elizabeth Peel and Damien Riggs (2010) *Lesbian, Gay, Bisexual, Trans and Queer Psychology: An Introduction*, Cambridge: Cambridge University Press.

Corrections Victoria, Department of Justice and Community Safety (2021) *Management of Prisoners who are Trans, Gender Diverse or Intersex* – March. Retrieved from: https://view.officeapps.live.com/op/view.aspx?src=https%3A%2F%2Ffiles. corrections.vic.gov.au%2F2021-06%2F2_63.docx&wdOrigin=BROWSELINK

De Beauvoir, Simone (1949) *The Second Sex*, Paris: Editions Gallimard.

Dernberger, Brittany (2017) "Limited Intersectional Approaches to Veteran and Former Prisoner Reintegration: Examining Gender Identity and Sexual Orientation", *Sociological Imagination*, 53(1): 42-62.

Duke, Karen (2003) *Drugs, Prisons and Policy-Making*, London: Palgrave Macmillan.

Gainsburg, Jeannie (2020) *The Savvy Ally: A Guide for Becoming a Skilled LGBTQI+ Advocate*, Maryland: Rowman and Littlefield.

Gorden, Caroline, Caroline Hughes and Edna Astbury-Ward (2017) "A Literature Review of Transgender People in Prison: An 'Invisible' Population in England and Wales", *Prison Service Journal*, 233: 11-22. Retrieved from: https://www.researchgate.net/publication/327184888_A_Literature_Review_of_Transgender_People_in_Prison_An_'invisible'_population_in_England_and_Wales

Hall, Elizabeth Lewis, Brad Christerson and Shelly Cunningham (2010) "Sanctified Sexism: Religious Beliefs and the Gender of Harassment of Academic Women", *Psychology of Women Quarterly*, 34(2): 181-185.

Harris, Mia (2017) "An insider's guide to being transgender in prison", *The Conversation* – May 17. Retrieved from: Https://theconversation.com-an-insiders-guide-to-being-transgender-in-prison-74970

Hoominfar, Elham (2021) "Gender Socialization", in Walter Leal Filho, Anabela Marisa Azul, Luciana Brandili, Amanda Lange Silvia, Tony Wall (eds.), *Gender Equality*, Switzerland: Springer, pp. 1-10.

Jouet, Mugambi (2021) "Foucault, Prison, and Human Rights: A Dialectic of Theory and Criminal Justice Reform", *Theoretical Criminology*, 26(2): 1-22.

Jumper, Shan (2021) "Issues in Working With Transgender Individuals Who Sexually Harm", *Sex and Gender Issues in Behavioral Health*, 23(42): 1-9.

Lamble, Sarah (2012) "Rethinking Gendered Prison Policies: Impacts on Transgender Prisoner", *ECAN Bulletin*, 16: 7-12. Retrieved from: https://howardleague.org/wp-content/uploads/2016/09/ECAN-Bulletin-16.pdf

Martino, Wayne (1999) "'Cool Boys', 'Party Animals', 'Squids' and 'Poofters': Interrogating the Dynamics and Politics of Adolescent Masculinities in School", *British Journal of Sociology of Education*, 20(2): 239-263.

Maycock, Matthew (2020) "The Transgender Pains of Imprisonment", *European Journal of Criminology*, 9(6): 1-21.

Melendez, Rita M. and Rogério Pinto (2007) "'It's Really a Hard Life': Love, Gender and HIV Risks Among Male-to-Female Transgender Persons", *Culture, Health & Sexuality*, 9(3): 233-245.

Meyer, Ilan H. (2003) "Prejudice, Social Stress, and Mental Health in Lesbian, Gay and Bisexual Populations: Conceptual Issues and Research Evidence", *Psychological Bulletin*, 129(5): 674-697.

Richardson, Diane (2015) "Conceptualising Gender", in Diane Richardson and Victoria Robinson (eds.), *Introducing Gender and Women's Studies*, Basingstoke: Palgrave Macmillan, pp. 1-16.

Rodgers, Jess, Nicole Asquith and Angela Dwyer (2017) "Cisnormativity, Criminalisation, Vulnerability: Transgender People in Prisons", *Tasmanian Institute of Law Enforcement Studies Briefing Paper*, 12: 1-13. Retrieved from: https://www.utas.edu.au/__data/assets/pdf_file/0004/944716/Briefing_Paper_No_12_J_Rodgers_N_Asquith_A_Dwyer.pdf

Singer, Benjamin (2013) "What is Transgender Studies for the Twenty-First Century?", in Susan Stryker and Aren Aizura (eds.), *The Transgender Studies Reader 2*, London: Routledge, pp. 1-18.

Smith, Nadine and Lily Trimboli (2010) *Comorbid Substance and Non-Substance Mental Health Disorders and Re-Offending Among NSW Prisoners*, Parramatta: NSW Bureau of Crime Statistics and Research – May. Retrieved from: https://www.bocsar.nsw.gov.au/Publications/CJB/cjb140.pdf

Stanley, Eric A., Dean Spade and Queer (In)Justice (2012) "Queering Prison Abolition, Now?", *American Quarterly*, 64(1): 115-127.

Sykes, Gresham (2007[1958]) *The Society of Captives: A Study of a Maximum Security Prison*, Princeton: Princeton University Press.

Testa, Rylan J., Janice Habarth, Jayme Peta, Kimberly Balsam and Walter Bockting (2015) "Development of the Gender Minority Stress and Eesilience Measure", *Psychology of Sexual Orientation and Gender Diversity*, 2(1): 65-77.

United Kingdom Legislation (2004) *Gender Recognition Act 2004*. Retrieved from: https://www.legilslation.gov.uk.ukpga/2004/7/contents

Victoria Legislation (1986) *Corrections Act 1986*. Retrieved from: https://www.legislation.vic.gov.au/in-force/statutes/corrections-act-1986

Victoria Legislation (2019) *Corrections Regulations 2019, Clause 86, 86(2G)*. Retrieved from: https://www.legislation.vic.gov.au/in-force/statutory-riles/corrections-regulations-2019/002

Wikberg, Stina (2013) "Art Education – Mostly for Girls? A Gender Perspective on the Art Subject in Swedish Compulsory School", *Education Inquiry*, 4(3): 577-593

Williams, Ian and Gary Winship (2018) "'Homeliness, hope and humour' (H³): Ingredients for Creation a Therapeutic Milieu of Prisons", *The International Journal of Therapeutic Communities*, 39(1): 4-13.

ABOUT THE AUTHOR

Dwayne Antojado is a researcher and academic with lived experience of the criminal justice system in Australia. He uses his lived experience to influence his research and advocacy work in academia, government, and the not-for-profit sector. He has led and worked on various projects embedding and amplifying lived experience perspectives in organisational practice, structure and processes with organisations including, the Australian Community Support Organisation, Jesuit Social Services, Vacro, and RMIT University's community-based and prison-based think tanks. Dwayne is currently an academic in the School of Social Sciences, Monash University, and La Trobe Law School, La Trobe University in Australia. He is also the Research Director for Humans of San Quentin, a story-telling project based in California, seeking to humanize the experiences of incarcerated people globally. His research interests include LGBTQI+ experiences in the justice system, lived experience criminology, education in prisons, and prison radio. He can be reached by email at dwayne.antojado@monash.edu or at the following address:

Dwayne Antojado
School of Social Sciences Menzies Building
20 Chancellors Walk
Monash University
Clayton VIC 3800, Australia

RESPONSE

Moving Beyond the Prison Pandemic: Reducing the Use and Harms of Imprisonment, Working Towards Decarceral Futures

Prison Pandemic Partnership in Collaboration with Sara Tessier, Patricia Whyte, Wendy Bariteau, Christophe Lewis, Deepan Budlakoti, Lindsay Jennings, Trish Mills, Sherri Maier-Gordon, Chantel Huel and Cathee Tkachuk

---

PREFACE

The following is an edited transcript from an event held online on 6 May 2023 entitled "Moving Beyond the Prison Pandemic: Reducing the Use and Harms of Imprisonment, Working Towards Decarceral Futures", which was transcribed by Olivia Gemma, who is a Research Assistant with the Prison Pandemic Partnership and Dialogue Editor for the *Journal of Prisoners on Prisons*. The event was organized by the Prison Pandemic Partnership, moderated by Kevin Walby (University of Winnipeg) and Justin Piché (University of Ottawa), and hosted by the University of Ottawa's Human Rights Research and Education Centre. The names of invited speakers are highlighted in bold and italics when they are first introduced to direct the reader's attention to their respective biographical statements.

INTRODUCTION

Kevin Walby: Welcome everyone to today's webinar, "Moving Beyond the Prison Pandemic: Reducing the Use and Harms of Imprisonment, Working Towards Decarceral Futures" hosted by the Human Rights Research and Education Centre based at the University of Ottawa. I'm Kevin Walby and I'm joining you today from Treaty One Territory, the traditional territory of the Anishinaabe, Cree, Oji-Cree, Dakota and Dene Peoples, and birthplace and homeland of the Métis Nation. I'm the director of the Centre for Access to Information and Justice at the University of Winnipeg, and an investigator for the Prison Pandemic Partnership.

Justin Piché: My name is Justin Piché and I'm joining you today from unceded and unsurrendered Algonquin Anishinaabe Terrritory as a member of the Criminalization and Punishment Education Project based at the

University of Ottawa and Carleton University, and as co-investigator for the Prison Pandemic Partnership.

Kevin Walby: March 11th, 2023 will mark three years since the COVID-19 pandemic was declared. Since the onset of COVID, congregate settings across Canada have been hard hit with infections by those living and working within them. This includes prisons where incarcerated people and staff have been infected at much higher rates than the general population based on the limited data that continues to be publicly disclosed about COVID-19 cases among imprisoned people.

These infections have grown year over year, as the pandemic has become normalized, and treated less like a public health emergency. Total reported cases among people in prison, in Canadian federal penitentiaries, nearly doubled from 1,336 cases by the end of February 2021 to 3,489 cases by the end of February 2022, and more than doubled again to 7,716 cases by the end of February this year.

During the initial wave of COVID-19, governments enacted several measures like emergency bail releases and expanded temporary absence programs (ETAs) with minimal harm and community benefits. This raised the possibility of ongoing diversion and decarceration to reduce the use of imprisonment, especially given that many governments failed to provide re-entry support to people exiting incarceration, despite calls from advocates and researchers to do so. These measures have largely now been rolled back, just as the paucity of re-entry support for criminalized people has persisted, undermining both public health and community safety in the process.

Throughout the pandemic governments have also introduced a whole lot of repressive measures to deal with COVID-19 in prison, like medical quarantines, isolation regimes often resembling segregation, suspension of programs, suspension of visits, putting in place lockdowns when outbreaks occur or are suspected, and so on.

And we've heard from lots of imprisoned people throughout the pandemic that this period has been marked by a lack of personal, protective equipment and cleaning and hygiene supplies, proportionate to the heightened risk posed by COVID-19 in these settings. At the same time, vaccine access and hesitancy among prisoners have emerged as a concern with varying vaccine take-up rates across jurisdictions signalling perhaps that some vaccine rollouts and communication strategies have been more effective than others.

Now, these are just a few of the issues that experts with lived experience of imprisonment and re-entry joining us today will speak on over the next two hours, and the Prison Pandemic Partnership has been documenting throughout COVID-19 with support from the Social Sciences and Humanities Research Council of Canada.

Let's now introduce our speakers from east to west. Thank you all very much for being here today. First, we welcome *Sara Tessier*, who's joining us from the ancestral and unceded Territory of the Mi'kmaq Peoples. Sara is a social justice advocate with lived experience who has spent the last seven years working with and on behalf of the most marginalized, victimized, criminalized, and institutionalized men, women, and youth in Canada. As the Impact Manager of Formerly Incarcerated Persons with the Northpine Foundation, she provides both financial and non-financial support to organizations in their efforts to increase successful reintegration to their beneficiaries and reduce recriminalization. Among the many other roles she has, Sara sits on the Lived Experience Committee for the Canadian Association of Elizabeth Fry Societies.

Next, we welcome *Patricia Whyte*, who's also joining us from the ancestral and unceded Territory of the Mi'kmaq Peoples. She's the first Indigenous peer support worker in Atlantic, Canada. She was the first regional manager of Holly House, which is a six-plex apartment building for Indigenous women. She's now employed with Path Legal as an advocate, and is involved in the Transformation, Voice and Systems Change working group with the Canadian Association of Elizabeth Fry Societies. Patricia is an Indigenous woman with lived experience, having served four years in the federal penitentiary system. Patricia is also a mother, sister, daughter, wife, teacher, and dedicated advocate for social change.

Justin Piché: We also have with us, *Wendy Bariteau*, from traditional unceded Mohawk Territory. Joanne Wendy Bariteau has worked for several organizations involved with supporting folks who are incarcerated and formally incarcerated across Canada. She's a member of the grassroots organization Joint Effort, a women's prisoner support group. She also helps with the Prison Justice Day Committee to organize public education, events, and prison justice network. She's now the regional coordinator for Ontario and Québec at the Canadian Association of Elizabeth Fry Societies, and she's also involved with other organizations such as the Anti-Carceral

Group and Abolition Coalition. Working in multiple regions has given her an appreciation for the federal carceral system and how it plays out in regional contexts.

Also joining us from traditional and unceded Mohawk Territory is *Christophe Lewis*, who's the founder of Freedom is a Must Foundation. Christophe was incarcerated for over 12 years. Having always had a passion for expressing himself through written and spoken word, he wrote poetry and music as a young man, and turned to journaling and keeping notes as a coping mechanism while in prison. Christophe was incarcerated in provincial institutions such as the Maplehurst Correctional Complex in Milton and the Don Jail in Toronto prior to his conviction, as well as Millhaven, Donnacona and Cowansville Institutions, and the Federal Training Centre. During his time in prison, he's experienced confinement at all levels of security. He's experienced segregation and involuntary transfer, and other harmful conditions. He's currently on day parole and lives in a transition house.

Next, we welcome *Deepan Budlakoti*, who is joining us from the unceded and unsurrendered Algonquin and Anishinaabe Territory. Deepan is an advocate for the human rights of prisoners and people, with precarious immigration status. He was released from the Ottawa-Carleton Detention Center (OCDC) over a year ago as a stateless person and is still waiting for federal government documents to be able to work. If you're interested in making a mutual aid contribution to Deepan to help cover the costs of housing, food, medication, transportation to appointments, including meetings he needs to attend to comply with his probation and immigration, as well as bail conditions, you can email justicefordeepan@gmail.com.

Next, is *Lindsay Jennings*, who's joining us from the traditional Territory of the Wendat, Anishinaabe, Haudenosaunee, and Mississaugas of the Credit First Nation, also known as Dish with One Spoon Territory. Lindsay has survived the prison system and is currently a research associate with the Tracking (In)justice Project, which tracks deaths by police using excessive force and deaths while incarcerated. She is the current co-chair of the Transition from Custody Network, working to address gaps in discharge planning and increase continuity of care for people moving in and out of the correctional system. She also chairs the Expert Advisory Committee for the Fresh Start Coalition, which is advocating for an automatic record suspension regime. Lindsay is a passionate and professional advocate for the human and healthcare rights of currently incarcerated individuals. Over the past years, Lindsay has been dedicated to addressing preventable deaths in custody and a more ethical, supportive, and compassionate process for the families of loved ones who have died behind bars.

We also have **Trish Mills**, who's a settler of mixed ancestry living in Southern Ontario, which has been and continues to be stewarded by the Haudenosaunee, Anishinaabe and Huron-Wendat, Erie and Chonnonton Peoples. Trish is an anarchist who is queer, neurodiverse, and disabled, and who has experienced both being in prison, as well as supporting others inside. She currently volunteers with the Disability Justice Network of Ontario, which is working to collectivize and amplify the voices and experiences of racialized and disabled prisoners, while providing concrete prisoner support.

Kevin Walby: We're also pleased **Sherri Maier-Gordon** is joining us from Treaty 4 and 6 Territory, and the traditional Territory of the Cree, Saulteaux and Assiniboine, and Métis Peoples. Sherri is a human justice graduate from the University of Regina and worked as a student with Correctional Services Canada (CSC) in the area of urban parole. Since graduation, she has dedicated her life to advocating for prisoners in both federal and provincial institutions. Over the past four years, she has been a prison wife and used education, professional, and personal experiences to help her fiancé and other families navigate the correctional system, especially during COVID-19. Together they organized, and held hunger strikes and protests in several Canadian carceral sites.

Also here with us is **Chantel Huel**, from Treaty 6 Territory in the homeland of the Métis. Chantel is a formerly incarcerated mother, grandmother, daughter, sister, partner, and friend. She is currently a helper and member with STR8 Up, and is on a journey to find greater balance and joy in her life and work by taking each day as it comes, using her voice and experiences to live honestly and with integrity.

Cathee Tkachuk is joining us from the traditional and unceded Territory of the Squamish, Musqueam, and Tsleil-Waututh First Nations. Cathee was in prison for 20 years and has been on parole for the last two, and dealt with the consequences of COVID-19 both inside and outside of prison.

PART I:
THE IMPACT OF COVID-19 ON PRISON
CONDITIONS AND COMMUNITY RE-ENTRY

Justin Piché: We have quite the lineup of speakers today who are going to share a lot of insights with us about the impact of the COVID-19 pandemic behind and beyond bars, and what we can do to work towards decarceral futures.

That brings us to our first question, where every speaker will have roughly up to five minutes each to respond in whatever way they feel relevant, based on their experience and where they're coming from. How did the COVID-19 pandemic impact prison conditions or community re-entry for you or those you advocate with and for?

To get us started, the first round is going to be east to west, and then the second round will be west to east. We'll start with Sara Tessier. Welcome.

Sara Tessier: Thank you, Justin. Good morning, everyone and welcome. I spent five years inside a federal prison and my release date was January 9th, 2020, just before the onset of the pandemic. I was released into a halfway house in Halifax.

As a prisoner inside, I was a peer advocate for the Elizabeth Fry Society. I took complaints, grievances – anything that the women needed, and advocated on their behalf. I also worked alongside Elizabeth Fry and Senator Kim Pate for systemic change.

Upon release going to the halfway house, I was still in contact with the people inside, so I could advocate on their behalf. When I was released, I was doing a lot of panel discussions. I was working as a volunteer with Nova Scotia Legal Aid. I was working with the Elizabeth Fry Society as well. I was out and about as much as I could be, as well as with my mandated programming through CSC.

When the pandemic hit and a state of emergency was declared, all of that was put to a halt. Although there were community restrictions, the halfway house took it above and beyond that. Where other people were allowed to go one person to the grocery store, we weren't allowed to leave the house at all. We couldn't even go for a walk around the block, so I would constantly be monitoring the conditions in that halfway house and working with Senator Kim Pate to address those.

Of course, inside the halfway houses, there's no access to the internet. Although I was able to meet and be interviewed by Ashley Avery of Coverdale Courtwork Society. By contacting her, she was able to get internet hubs from the library for the halfway house, which was good because we were able to access our programming remotely. Although, it didn't address the fact that you were imprisoned in a house now. It's no different than being in the prison and it was very restrictive.

Inside the prison, through my advocacy work, the restrictions were extremely harsh, and I was always speaking with the Inmate Committee Chair to monitor those conditions and report them. Protective equipment like masks, gloves, and cleaning supplies weren't provided to the people incarcerated. It was only the staff that were wearing masks and gloves around. The staff were the only ones that would be bringing the virus in and prisoners had no contact with anybody on the outside. Visits were restricted to non-existent and programming stopped, which greatly impacted people close to parole or needing that mandated program to get parole. People were being kept inside longer than their original date for parole, which really created a backlog. Not to mention, all non-essential staff were no longer going into the prisons and now you had simple things like food services, hygiene, all these services and things that people needed daily, even medication, restricted. People weren't getting the mental health services or anything they really needed. Now they exacerbate people's mental health issues and provided less or no support for those who really needed it. It was very detrimental and harmful to people, which leads me to the work I started doing outside with the JEC Project, which I'll get into later on.

Justin Piché: Alright! Thank you so much for that, Sara. We'll come back to you later. We're now going to turn the floor over to Patricia. Welcome!

Patricia Whyte: Hi! First of all, I'd like to say I'm super honoured to be on an amazing panel with some fantastic speakers and advocates. I want to start off on the cultural side – Sara and I know each other very well and we've worked together quite a bit. My warrant expiry was in September 2020 and I was already working for Elizabeth Fry as a peer support worker then. We had what was called down here as "People's Park" and it was filled with tents. As Sara was explaining about the JEC Program, it was John Howard, Elizabeth Fry, and Coverdale that came together and we had all this funding for hotels for the women and men, which caused a lot of issues. The sweats stopped in the community because even though we had an Elder willing to do the sweats, the parole officers weren't allowing their clients to sweat because they felt like it was too serious. I've had COVID four times even being vaccinated. I've never stopped working even through the whole thing. I think there was no sense of stability. There was no sense of consistency in terms of programming support. It was chaos.

All the programming stopped even with the cultural base. People couldn't smudge together and the Healing Circle stopped. It was like Sara was saying, mental health was on a decline.

I also worked at Holly House, which is one of our supportive living houses, and some positives came into that because they were trying to push everybody out of the provincial centres who didn't have extreme charges on their record. They got to come out. We had a few women who were charged with first-degree murder and worked on their case, and they got to stay in the community instead of prison.

I also had a partner who recently just got released on January 31st. He did four years in the provincial system and they wouldn't go to the doctor if they had a sore throat. Nobody on the range would because as soon as they mentioned anything about a sickness, they would get locked down for days. They didn't have the proper equipment – no PPE, never got masks, nothing, no healthcare at all. It was terrible.

Justin Piché: Alright. Thank you, Patricia. We'll now turn the floor over to Christophe. Are you here? Go ahead!

Christophe Lewis: I'm here. Hello, everybody! My name is Christophe Lewis and I did 12 years inside. I was released in November 2021 and, last April, I was granted full parole.

I've been working in the community with whatever organizations would hire me because getting employment is another difficult thing when you have a criminal record, especially one like mine. By the way, I'm serving a life sentence. For those that don't know what that means, I'm going to be under surveillance and CSC-watch for the rest of my life, according to the law that is set right now.

I was released during the pandemic, so I can speak to how things were while I was there. All visits were halted, which meant that not only family visitors couldn't come, but we weren't able to have visits from prison psychologists either. Sometimes parole officers (POs) weren't even allowed to come to see us, which slowed down our reintegration processes on all different levels. Forget about programs, there was no such thing at the time when the pandemic had hit. For all those that didn't do programs or needed programs, they weren't able to be afforded those rights. Obviously, that's a big hindrance to the process and the way things operate.

There was so much that was actually going on. There were constant random lockdowns, for instance, a staff member would say something simple like, "Oh, you know, I think I was in contact with someone that may have had COVID". They just "may have had COVID", but they aren't saying that some did have COVID. And then they wouldn't be able to come into the institution and anybody that was in contact with them now had to be included. So, you know, some people would say that the staff members are doing this because they wanted hazard pay, and obviously when there's hazard pay, they get paid a lot more.

A lot of times, we would get locked down for ridiculous reasons. One of the things that we would point out as prisoners is that when these so-called staff members would say that they were in contact with someone that possibly had COVID, we would have to do 14 days of quarantine. Yet, they would come back to work within days and then we would still be in quarantine. We'd have to submit three negative PCR tests. Until then, we'd be segregated. We wouldn't have visits. We wouldn't have anything. I would say that it was a difficult thing to navigate on all different levels and I wouldn't wish that on my worst enemy. And it still happens to this day. There's still random lockdowns, no matter how the prison restrictions have eased. There's still a lot of arbitrary lockdowns, I would say.

Justin Piché: Alright. Thanks so much, Christophe, for sharing your experiences of the pandemic behind bars. We're going to turn the floor over now to Deepan Budlakoti. Deepan, the floor is yours.

Deepan Budlakoti: Thank you everyone for inviting me to this event today. I will be speaking solely on my experiences while held at the Ottawa-Carleton Detention Centre (OCDC). I spent four and a half years in pretrial custody and was released on February 24th, 2022. I was held at OCDC prior to COVID and then throughout the outbreaks. I personally got COVID one time in custody and then one time outside of custody.

The changes that took place during COVID were essentially around lockdown. They classify lockdown as in COVID lockdowns, medical lockdown, or just a lockdown. Essentially all are forms of segregation with the same experience in terms of forced isolation. We don't have access to visitors. We don't have access to any type of programming. We weren't able to have any type of PPE until a year went by during COVID, and finally we were allowed to get a mask only when leaving the unit. This also hindered the ability to see the psychologist. Mental health support declined during the time of COVID. Instead of increasing care, we were in forced isolation for long periods of time. For example, it could be 28 to 38 days. Sometimes we were only released for one to three hours, and then the whole process would start again.

Several things did change in terms of quality. The quality of food deteriorated significantly. Portions got smaller. Instead of getting a container, we started getting little cardboard dishes. At times, there were months and months when we weren't able to get fresh air. As some of you may be aware at OCDC, a provincial institution, you don't have access to a window. In particular, at OCDC, you're in a cell where you cannot see outside of the window. There are times when you are with one or two cell partners. You're sleeping on a two-inch matt and no pillow. You have an open-seat toilet with no air filtration that's going through the cell. Before COVID, compared to during COVID, nothing changed in terms of hygiene and cleaning solutions that are provided to the units. In addition to that, while you're locked down and someone is positive, the whole unit is then locked down. When that same individual would leave the unit to take a shower and individuals that weren't positive planned to also use the shower, the staff wouldn't clean those showers. One shower for 24 prisoners or one shower for 36 prisoners, depending on how many cells are on that unit or how many people are in each cell.

There are ongoing issues in terms of programming, getting access to visits and mail, and simply the canteen. We essentially went from having some access to fresh air and support to absolutely nothing. They say they invested hundreds of millions of dollars during COVID to help individuals reintegrate into society, and it seems all fine and dandy by what's expressed by [then Solicitor General] Sylvia Jones in the media or press conferences. In reality, nothing was being done on the frontlines. We were in lockdown again, pretty much the same thing as segregation. I define it as forced isolation as there's no difference, and you're putting everyone at risk.

There was no ability to social distance. Walking parameters are essentially six feet. There are assigned benches and tables on one side. You're living in a hallway setting and you don't have access to fresh air. The correctional officers will come and go. It was consistent lockdowns. I don't even know how to express it. You're already going through a hard time while you're incarcerated. You'd think that the state would provide you support to help you deal with the matter and now you don't even have the proper information. You're not getting access to what's happening with COVID.

And that is my five-minute mark. I'll end by saying that incarceration during COVID isn't something I would wish upon anyone. There were inhumane and deplorable conditions in pretrial custody at OCDC in the nation's capital city of Ottawa. Thank you.

Justin Piché: Alright. Thanks so much, Deepan, for sharing your insights. We'll now go to Wendy Bariteau. The floor is yours.

Wendy Bariteau: Hi! When COVID-19 started and we started seeing restrictions within the institution, our fear – well, my fear – was that the restrictions put in place might not be 100 percent removed at the end of the pandemic or when things went back to "normal". This is what we are seeing. A lot of what was once given, including visits, ETAs [Escorted Temporary Absences], and on-time documentation, like what everybody else is talking about, would ideally be coming back to pre-pandemic standards. We're not seeing that in everything. ETAs, in a lot of institutions designated for women, are still not up. They're saying they need to retrain volunteers and some institutions are waiting until September and October, so folks aren't getting ETAs because they have no volunteers to take them out. And in some places, movements are still restricted.

Personnel are still working from home, so some folks aren't meeting up with their POs [parole officers] or their personal support workers [PSW] as often as they should. The institution is not 100 percent back to pre-pandemic standards and they're not even doing community standards now. Federal and provincial governments are almost all back to normal, but the federal institutions, so CSC, is still in pandemic mode. There's still some quarantines happening and movement restrictions at times, which may happen if there's a few outbreaks or a lot of them.

For institutions designated for women and CSC as a whole, they're not post-pandemic. They're still in pandemic mode, be that as not as intensive, but still so. It can be problematic for people that are requesting parole that haven't gotten ETAs. I've heard people that are having private or family visits, then have to be put in quarantine once their family or private visit is done. A lot of people aren't wanting to go through all that or not taking advantage of the private or family visits. Also, some institutions are down to one visit a month or one visit a week. I would hope that soon we will see a post-pandemic that looks exactly like the pre-pandemic in the institutions, and that would be the ultimate goal to go back to community standards. What's happening in communities should be implemented in federal institutions.

Justin Piché: Thank you, Wendy. A good reminder in terms of just how much has changed behind bars and in the community. Despite the fact that the pandemic has been normalized in other industries and sectors, the pandemic continues for those living and working in congregate settings, and in this case congregate settings of human caging. So we'll now turn the floor over to Lindsay Jennings.

Lindsay Jennings: Thanks, Justin. I just want say thanks to the organizers. It's pretty cool and very rare that you get to share space with so many people with lived experience. Thank you for organizing this.

I think for myself, being involved in the Tracking (In)justice Project where my contribution is really around deaths in custody. With everything that everybody was just talking about of the conditions that happened inside during the pandemic, what we saw was a dramatic increase in deaths inside. There's been two reports in the past four months that have come out. The first report was back in December from the Tracking (In)justice Project about deaths in custody in our Ontario provincial jails. When they compared deaths in 2021 to 2010, there was a 173 percent increase in deaths inside of our provincial jails during our pandemic times. Some people would think, "Oh, they probably got COVID", though, there were maybe only two or three folks whose deaths were actually linked to COVID.

More recently, a new report came out that was led by the Chief Coroner of Ontario, who wanted to bring to light some issues within the provincial correctional system that contributed to this alarming increase in deaths.

That report came out at the end of January or February, I believe. I want to give you some numbers, and though numbers don't necessarily mean anything to me, it seems to mean a lot to funders and the government. That's kind of why I got into research – I wanted to change the way that we were using research in order to push for social change and really challenge some of the policies and processes within the correctional system. I know it's really important that we understand the demographics of how people have died and the environment within our provincial correctional system.

74 people between 2014 and 2021 died from drug toxicity, meaning they overdosed inside. We had 45 people die from suicide, 12 were undetermined, and 3 were so-called accidents. One of the most alarming numbers was 52 people, which was 28 percent of deaths between 2014 and 2021 were deemed natural causes. That's a large portion of people inside that are dying from so-called natural causes. These are young folks between 25 and 40. We shouldn't have young folks dying at that rate inside our provincial jails.

When you ask me this question about what did the pandemic do to people – it killed people inside. COVID didn't – the conditions people were in did. People's mental health deteriorated and that's why we saw suicide increase. We have lockdowns directly associated with an increase in deaths and the deterioration of people's mental health. No visits, no programs, and lockdowns constantly. I think it's important to remember the way that people are living inside. During COVID, we had fridges and TVs, we had Zoom things – everything moved and transformed into COVID life. Imagine if you were stuck in your bathroom and if you have a bathtub that's your bed. If you don't have a bathtub, you put some pillows down on the ground. That's what people are living in for 23 and a half hours a day. That naturally is going to affect people. Like, we're still humans. People inside are human beings.

We've been affected in the community by COVID. We're talking about our brain fog, talking about burnout exhaustion, social anxiety that picked up, depression, and deaths by suicide increased out here. Folks inside are humans. The Chief Coroner's report identified two major contributing factors to the deaths: staff shortages and lockdowns, and non-compliance from officers and correctional staff. That's really important too. We keep pushing for accountability. We have information that non-compliance is one of the biggest reasons and contributors to people not getting the healthcare and crisis response that they deserve in a time of crisis.

We have officers refusing to give Naloxone. We have officers refusing to answer the distress button inside the cell. I'd like to end off with this – we have control of our life out here, for the most part. And for the most part, even through the pandemic, we had choice. People have the choice to get vaccines. People have the choice to wear masks. Inside you didn't have a choice of what to do with anything. You can't protect yourself inside, you're defenceless inside. I do think it's really important that we don't get caught up in what's happening in our community. If you do this work and if you're an advocate for folks inside, we really need to remember that they're living in basically bathroom stalls. They haven't been given masks, 23 and a half hour lockdowns, no fresh air, no sunshine, no interaction, and no connection. With all of those contributing factors, you're not going to have healthy human beings, and that contributes to their death sentences.

One really small thing, 70% of the folks have died inside during 2021 were on remand. When that links to re-entry, these folks didn't even get an opportunity to enter back into the community. They went in there waiting for bail and they came out to their families, children, and loved ones in a body bag.

Justin Piché: Thank you for sharing your insights, Lindsay. Almost three years ago, in the spring, a number of groups across the country had organized a caravan remarking this pandemic would lead to more deaths by incarceration, and that effectively we would have a death penalty by another name. A number of folks thought that was just over the top language, but we've just seen heard how much prison has killed during this pandemic. We'll now move to our next speaker. Trish Mills, the floor is yours.

Trish Mills: Thank you. I'll be speaking a little bit from personal experience, as well as advocacy experience. I'll start with my own story, which is that I was arrested during the COVID pandemic somewhat early on and over the course of an all-day contested hearing, ended up being released on an incredibly strict house arrest, which was no absence from my house even for medical or personal reasons, including groceries. The only reason that I was given that release was because of COVID, which isn't a credit.

Yes, I've been inside. I've been sentenced to prison, but I'm actually very grateful that I was in my house. House arrest lasts for a total of 18 months – and to be clear, 18 months of not being allowed to leave your home is longer than a lot of sentences pre-COVID that individuals got for sexual assault, negligence causing death, and things like that. Again, this isn't at all a call for harsher sentences or even "a woe was me". I'm just trying to create a pointed comparison of how fundamentally messed up the outcome was in and around COVID and the courts, even in the most minor cases.

All in all, that had a profound impact on both my mental health, as well as my physical health. Ultimately, it wasn't even the Crown that ended the sentence or resolved the situation. I actually forced a new bail hearing by requesting that my surety withdraw their support, which forced a new bail hearing in front of a new judge. During that time of COVID, house arrest was also subjected to hyper-surveillance by police and harassment. Lots of police driving by, parking in front of my house, calling to me when I was on the porch, just making it very clear that they let me go, but they're also actively looking for any reason to put me back in, which is, of course, how police regularly treat people and communities who are Black, Indigenous, and poor.

I'm also speaking a little bit today on behalf of the Disability Justice Network of Ontario and some advocacy I did for a prisoner support project during the first six months. I did some noise demos to try and make sure imprisoned people knew that they weren't alone, which was during the COVID mandate and lockdowns. Later on, I ended up hearing a lot from prisoners through the Disability Justice Network of Ontario on support lines. I would say my biggest takeaway from that is just as other people pointed out, that COVID-19 impacted prisoners in many ways. If you don't get sick or die, you face court delays, you face extended lockdowns, segregation, the cancellation of visits and yard, which overall we got the sense that there was a lot of frustration. I'd also say that after speaking with folks, one of the biggest harm of COVID-19 on prisoners was the increased fear of isolation.

Using this as a prompt for people watching today or in the future to remember back to where you were and how you felt in March 2020, with media stations broadcasting images of hospitals with overworked staff speaking about having to make choices on who lives or dies, emergency army triage tents in parking lots, body bags, grave digging, recordings of people collapsing in the street. This was a time of wiping down your groceries with Lysol and trying to maintain some semblance of control and sanity over the situation, but you remember the palpable fear, tension, and panic that you felt and experienced at the grocery stores, and throughout all of this. Now, imagine experiencing all of that locked in a small, overcrowded cage with terrible air quality, and having no control over the people coming in and out of your range, whether they're bringing in this dangerous disease, intentionally or unintentionally. Not given access to any masks or cleaning supplies, and not even knowing if you'd receive appropriate medical care – all of that in isolation.

No visits, no phone calls, trouble getting in touch with lawyers, no word from the courts, leaving you with the impression that nobody cares, that nobody is listening to you, and that somehow, even you yourself, think you deserve it. I think those feelings and experiences were exponentiated, which is probably the biggest takeaway that I've received from talking to folks who have experienced prison sentences during those times.

Justin Piché: Alright. Thank you, Trish, for sharing your experiences of being in the community during this pandemic, while being criminalized, as well as sharing your work with the Disability Justice Network of Ontario. We're now going to shift to Sherri Maier-Gordon. The floor is now yours. Go ahead.

Sherri Maier-Gordon: I don't even know where to start. As an advocate, I was very busy. As a prison wife, I went through a lot of battles. The advocacy work eventually ended up making my fiancé a target for a lot of things that we spoke about at the beginning. There was no PPE [personal protective equipment] when we were over at Saskatchewan Penitentiary. I'm kind of going to limit some of the information because we're already a target once again for where we're at right now.

We had court battles in 2020. We had our appeal that caused a battle for us just having to do everything through video court. Visits were the biggest battle for us. We've been together for almost four years. Probably for a good two and a half years it was stuck really down to video visits. A lot of those video visits got cancelled because there were lockdowns and they couldn't leave off the range. Once, we ended up going to Alberta prison. I will note, we've been to four institutions in four years. We're finally on the fourth one when we did start to get open visits. We got hit numerous times with the ion scanners and those became a big battle for us because it prevented us from actually having contact. I think it was around last year when Edmonton Maximum Institution started to open up their visits, we constantly hit on the ion scanners. Where most people were able to have no issues getting in and touching their loved ones, it took us over a year to actually do that. We believe that a lot of that had to do with the advocating that he and I did. And programming, too, specifically mental health-wise, Dr. Piché knows because I've shared my story with him. He helped us to try to get my fiancé to go somewhere that would help with his mental health issues because they weren't being addressed. It took over a year to actually get my fiancé to a place where he could have those issues addressed. Now that he's in a psych centre, he's getting that help.

Prior to that, they just didn't have the ability to do it. Psychologists weren't coming to work. Parole officers weren't coming to work and were working from home. On an advocate level, I know in some institutions like Edmonton Max, POs just weren't working at all. You were seeing a lot of prisoners that were stuck in a maximum setting for seven to eight years. I hope that we never see an issue like this again because as a "lifer wife" it's hard when you have to go through these things. Mental health-wise and all the lockdowns, they have caused a lot of grief. I've literally sat on the phone when my fiancé has decided to slash up. I could hear the guards in the background telling him to drop the blade, and he's threatening to slash his throat and then the phone just getting shut right off. I think that I can handle that in a better way than most people could because of the advocacy that I do.

I've seen more things in the three years of the pandemic that I don't think I'd ever want to see and I would never wish them on anybody, like nobody at all. It's been stressful to not be able to sometimes have your loved one call because they've been on a 20-day lockdown. I remember at Saskatchewan Pen, there was a time they were only out for a half hour and it came down to the point where my fiancé would say, "do I call home to my wife or take a shower?" Sometimes he and other guys were taking bird baths in their sinks in their cells. It becomes really a hard thing when you're so used to having visits on a regular basis. I mean, yes, before COVID we did. We had visits constantly, two times a week when we were in the maximum institution. When we went down to medium, we were at one hour once a week on video visits to going down to nothing. Prisoners like a sense of a pattern and routine, and it just impacts a lot of what was going on. It definitely affected his mental health in many ways.

I've advocated on the provincial level with people like the late Cory Cardinal. Even on the provincial level, there are a lot of problems that were inside, including the living conditions. Some units didn't have cells, so they lived in dorms and the conditions were just horrible. Guards weren't wearing masks either. They weren't giving inmates masks. They weren't keeping conditions clean. Women at the Pine Grove Institution weren't getting any kind of cleaner to clean anything with. And again, I've seen so many people that have suffered from severe mental health issues worse with COVID than prior to COVID, and my fiancé is one of those. It's sad because he used to be a really happy person. Me advocating has made us a huge target within the prison system right down from every institution we went to that he really worries about standing up and doing things like advocating for himself. I've had to zip my lip since COVID just to make sure things don't get worse for him or for us, or even for other people. Some people have told me, sometimes advocating since COVID has really put a target on a lot of people and I find it very unfortunate.

I really do hope that they have better means for mental health and improve them now that people are starting to realize what the damages are from the pandemic.

Justin Piché: Alright. Thank you, Sherri, for sharing your experience and for the work that you have been doing for folks where you're from. It's been really, really important work, and everyone here thanks you for your advocacy. So, next we'll go to Chantel Huel. The floor is now yours.

Chantel Huel: Good morning, everybody. I was granted day parole on March 11th, 2020, and that evening the world pandemic hit and everything was locked down. I remember being in the institution at Edmonton Institution for Women. Volunteers had come in from the outside and that was the last I had ever seen volunteers again. We were immediately locked down in our units. I've seen a lot of mental health deterioration because nobody had movement. It was obviously modified movements. We were given an hour out each day to use the phone and to go for a walk outside, but I was just waiting for transportation and I was released on April 8th, 2020 back into the community. They couldn't find transportation because no buses were running and no flights going out, so two chaplains from Edmonton Institution for Women actually drove me from Edmonton to Saskatoon.

I listen to some of the stories from the east to west coast, and my stories weren't that harsh. We still had movement, we were still allowed out. We still had access to programming and we still had access to psychology. I stayed in the halfway house for five months and then I was released on statutory release, so I got my own place.

I've served two federal sentences before this one. This is my third one, and for me I suffer from PTSD, anxiety, and social anxiety disorder because of the trauma that I went through before this federal sentence. When I was talking to Sherry yesterday, I said, "I think I have a different perspective on this and it helped me to reintegrate into society, not saying that it's a good thing, but for me, it was a good thing". It was slow-moving. I work at STR8 UP – 10,000 Little Steps to Healing. It's the only gang exit program of its kind in Saskatchewan. Some of the things that we've faced working with our members and our piece on the inside is deterioration of mental health. Obviously being put into quarantine, only being allowed out for half an hour each day – it's either you take that shower or you make that phone call or somebody's taking a shower and some cellmates are making the phone call for them.

Violence is increased in institutions because of the pandemic and lockdowns. People are fighting over the craziest stuff, and I think to what Sherry said – I'll piggy back on that – there's no cleaning supplies that were provided for us on the inside. The guards were provided everything they needed from masks to gloves to wipes to cleaning supplies, and there were tape lines put out, and we weren't allowed to cross them in case we were going to give them COVID. But the funny thing is, we always said, "you're the ones that leave and you come back every day". We don't have the ability to leave and go out into the public where we're gonna catch this virus, and bring it back. Just treated worse than ever. Just a lot of mental health deterioration and an increase in violence.

And what did they take away? They took away the culture from us. They took away mental health support on the inside. They took away all the volunteers and support that would come in and spend their time with you, so that you could move forward in a better way. Now you're stuck with your housemates or locked in your cell and confined. Yeah, the conditions got worse. I remember they tried to get us stuff that would keep us occupied and keep our minds busy, but you can only be around the same people for so long and insanity sets in. I guess my story is just a little bit different because it was more supportive for me and I still had access to stuff here in Saskatoon once I was released from prison. Thank you.

Justin Piché: Thank you, Chantel. I think it's an important reminder to point out that there are a lot of common experiences throughout the pandemic, but there's unevenness as well. I do thank you for your remarks. Now, we'll turn the floor over to Cathee Tkachuk. The floor is yours.

Cathee Tkachuk: Hi, everybody! Thank you for having me today. Oh, my gosh! There are so many things that were so similar for me. Just to quickly go with what happened on the inside, we didn't have work, we didn't have visitors, and we were locked up every day except for an hour. Now, that's with the same eight people, in the same house, in the same setting every single day. The cleaning supplies were also an issue. When the pandemic wasn't there, we would get up and go to work. We did our thing. We weren't there all day, most of us, anyway. The same amount of cleaning supplies and even toilet paper and things like that just don't cut it when everybody is at home. We don't have extra things during this pandemic, however, the guards would come in and do a cleaning supply check to make sure there were two bottles here and two bottles there, but the bottles weren't increased. They just had to be in different places, which I found amusing and super sad.

Christophe, you reminded me I had to be taking a note for an acute health experience and when I came back I was quarantined for 14 days. The staff, who brought me back, was doing rounds the next day. I did my 14 days and the person who was out exactly the same amount of time was back at work the next day. Also, ETAs were gone, so there was no reintegration. It was just boom!

I did 22 years. I came in 1999 and got out in 2021 with no ETA and no reintegration. Luckily, I got my parole and that's wonderful. I'm not complaining about that. I feel, though, that nobody could really give me an example of what I should be doing out there because the pandemic was new. What are the halfway house choices? What happens if somebody there gets sick? By the way, I got COVID three times. I was locked in my room, and I could not come out, except to use the washroom. I couldn't do my laundry. I couldn't associate with anybody and luckily I was out, so I still had my computer and phone, but I had to depend on the halfway house staff to bring me food, and you know the halfway house is a busy place. I spent a lot of money on Uber Eats. My family lives in Medicine Hat, so they were helping me financially.

Emotionally, it was very difficult though. It felt like you were alone out here. You were in your room and you have no access to even water except to go to the bathroom. I don't know about you, but I don't like filling up my water in the bathroom. It's a thing with me, so I felt like I didn't have access to water. We would have to depend on the staff and they would leave the item outside the door. Your medications in the morning would be left outside the door in a little cup or your tea that you would ask for, or whatever it was that you needed. While you were stuck for six days inside your room. I guess my subconscious is trying to distance me personally from that because it was pretty traumatic. I just got out from doing 22 years and here I was stuck in a room, and I found that pretty concerning.

I just thank you so much for having us here. I have so many things that I could bring up. One last thing that happened in there that was super difficult for me was I lived in a program unit and it was a pretty intense program, and the staff showed up and said, "grab your stuff, you're moving to house 10. We need this area because these are the only rooms that lock from the outside and this is going to be used as a COVID unit". So, essentially they're locking people in from the outside in a small unit, in a cement building, and displacing everybody that lived in that building to a different house. Same thing happened when we were in minimum. The minimum unit is quite a ways' away from the medium compound in Abbotsford, so the staff showed up one day and said, "you have 15 minutes. Grab an overnight bag, you're going back to medium operational difficulties". That meant that everything that you had and all the people, stability, and routine that you had built inside was gone. The medium compound was a bunch of us who had earned our minimum security status and it was challenging on so many levels.

People bring up mental health –and I'm sorry I'm looking at my timer. People bring up mental health issues and I had mental health issues before I went to prison. My mental health issues in prison were exacerbated so severely when I was in there during COVID that it seemed like everything was closing in. I had to talk to my PO on the telephone and that's if I could even get a hold of her. After getting out after decades, your PO is going up for you to supposedly speak for you at the parole hearing and you haven't had any ETAs. Luckily, I got my parole, but I hit the streets kind of not grounded in any way, and that severely affected my reintegration. Thank you so much for having me.

PART II:
BUILDING COMMUNITIES TO IMPROVE
THE OUTCOMES OF ALTERNATIVES TO
IMPRISONMENT

Kevin Walby: Thank you, Cathee and thanks to all of our speakers for being open and just being vulnerable. To share some of the experiences you've had, and share the pain that you've felt and your reflections on the COVID-19 pandemic harms of imprisonment and re-entry.

Now, we're going to turn to a second question and we'll go in the reverse order. Drawing on your experience, what's one key support that governments and community members should invest in to improve outcomes of bail and prison releases for criminalized people in ways that will enhance community well-being and safety? We'll come back to you Cathee.

Cathee Tkachuk: I think that a peer-driven advocacy program for every parolee should be implemented, meaning when I get out of prison I'll have somebody who knows what it's like to be incarcerated in a federal or provincial or whatever carceral setting. That person is there for me and only me, not the 19 other people in my halfway house. That person is the person who is going to help me get stable, literally, and I'm talking about things that seem so small to other people. Getting my identifications, how to take the train, get introduced to people in the community, and setup banking and finances. Not like not giving money, but taking people to the bank, taking people to whatever office they need to go to for financial support. And it should be peer-driven because we're the only people who know what it's like. That's somebody with who you could develop a rapport with and trust. That's somebody who knows where you are, knows what might be hard for you, knows what's going on in your life, and how incredibly trying coming onto the street is! It would also create employment for the peers who are doing the advocacy.

It would be an amazing program and that should be nationwide, and it shouldn't be just federal or provincial. It can be anybody coming out of an intense carceral situation. I feel like that would help people exponentially compared to what we have now, which is virtually nothing. Yeah, I think our people could help our people and then educate other people and, hopefully, we could build a big network like that of help, hope, and support. Thank you.

Kevin Walby: Thank you, Cathee. That's a very good idea. Thanks for bringing up the idea of peer mentoring and recognizing that people have incredible skills to help people survive. Thanks for recognizing all that. Okay, continuing with this question, we'll go back to Chantel.

Chantel Huel: Cathee just stole everything I needed to say. No, I'm just kidding, Cathee. I love you so much. Everything Cathee spoke to, we actually do this out of the organization that I work at. We have an office at Saskatchewan Penitentiary. We go into all the correctional centres in Saskatchewan. We have lived experience of people that have been through the systems. Not pushing others and not pulling them, but walking beside them and leading the way with them.

One thing that we might want to work on is having more spots available for these people to get released and get bail. We need bail workers in the institutions to build relationships in a healthy way with people who have lived experience. I always say, "there's nothing about us, without us". Somebody from a textbook can't speak to my life because they have no idea what I've been through, right? Prisons should be willing to have people with lived experience working on bail plans with the people residing there. Like Cathee said, she nailed it – who better to help somebody coming out of it than somebody who's been through it with anxieties, fears, and unknowns? Holding their hand and walking beside them, and just leading the way in a positive light. It was people with lived experiences that helped me reintegrate every time. I'm a slow learner and it took me a few times to get it, but here I am. I got it and now I'm leading the way for others.

Kevin Walby: Thank you so much, Chantel. Thank you for all the work that you're doing. We'll go back to this question now with Sherri.

Sherri Maier-Gordon: I just think that there needs to be more programs in general. I look back at the programs my fiancé was taking and, as a lifer, it's a lot harder for him to take some of the programs. As an advocate, I have seen other people that had told me, especially in the federal system, they would start a program and then it was cut halfway through. We've seen a lot of this with COVID.

I almost can't believe that I'm going to give some praise to Edmonton Max right now, but I was actually talking with my fiancé this morning about programs and he reminded me of how there was a program that helped people suffering from addictions. They actually did a televised program at Edmonton Max for some substance abuse programs. I think doing things like that, just allowing more programs inside will help people get bail and parole because a lot of times people come up for bail or parole, and the reason they can't get released is because they have issues such as addictions. I worry if we win an appeal with my fiancé, what kinds of hurdles are they going to put in front if him? I'm grateful, though, that we're at an institution now where he's getting extreme amounts of programs. Even during COVID, the Regional Psychiatric Centre is actually one place where we didn't see a lot of lockdowns. I think we've been there now for eight months and we've seen one, and it only lasted for a couple of days. They're really heavy on programming and trying to set these guys up to get what they need, so they can be released and integrated into the community.

As an advocate, I've seen the struggles that some people face and one of them is not being able to get into the right programs or not having enough spots in a program. If you're somebody who's doing a longer sentence, you don't get your programming until the end of your sentence and that becomes a challenge because then they're scrambling around trying to get you into that program. I also think there just needs to be more funding for a lot of the programs for people that are incarcerated.

Kevin Walby: Thank you, Sherri. Thank you for all those points. Next, we're going to go back to Trish.

Trish Mills: I thought about this question a lot and went in maybe a little different direction. Basically, most of the people that we talk to and support through the Disability Justice Network are both racialized and disabled. They're people who've been failed by many systems for most of their lives, and whose criminalization is sometimes less about what they've done and more about the implicitly racist and ableist systems that make up our society.

The reality is that one singular support program isn't likely to improve the bail or release outcome of someone like that who's facing such disproportionate systemic forces. What it would take is the dismantling of the white supremacist systems that put and keep them there in the first place. So, what then?

My answer is for individuals, academics, and professionals to invest more in the well-being and safety of our communities, which include prisoners and those who are criminalized. Prison abolition needs more of our time, more of our dreams, more of our trust, and more of our intentions. And I say abolition to mean nothing short of the complete decarceration of all prisoners. Also building care and community-centred approaches to accountability and justice. I say it also to mean actively creating supports and programs that intentionally support abolition as the ultimate long-term goal. No more stop gaps that also support or expand the prison industrial complex or surveillance state. Nothing that can inadvertently be used to justify putting more people in cages any longer.

We know that prisons don't work. We know they don't prevent or reduce crime because they don't address the roots of it. They don't contribute to community safety because our carceral systems create more violence. They don't rehabilitate that. They aren't containers that deliver ethical care. I and the people I support are really ready for something different and, in fact, need it. So, my proposal is abolition.

Kevin Walby: Thank you, Trish. You really put that very well and articulated a great vision of the kind of politics of people working in the area. Thank you very much for your comments. Next, we're going to go to Wendy.

Wendy Bariteau: Thank you so much for having me. Everything that Trish said – as an abolitionist, I concur. Instead of thinking of how we can get folks out of institutions, how can we stop them from getting into institutions? We're talking about the decriminalization of sex workers and drug use, ending minimum sentencing, bail hearings, and decriminalization of minority groups and gender-diverse people. We're talking about First Nations' peoples. We're talking Black, queer, and transgender women.

The starting point is having fewer and fewer people that are sentenced and doing jail time, and moving in the direction of abolition – of not having jails and not having people put into cages. We're not helping any community when we take people out of their own community and put them in jail and pretend that we're helping. I'm not saying these people, but us people, because I'm also serving in my sentence. Putting people in jail and then expecting us to come back well physically and emotionally – that's not how it works.

My experiences with the federal system, and as a personal view, I did not come out of jail better than when I went in CSC. It didn't necessarily help me. I took the eight years I was incarcerated to help myself. If I would have had the services necessary pre-incarceration, it would have made a lot of difference. The tools weren't there to help me with my issues, which were addiction and mental health issues. I didn't have the tools to do that. The system didn't provide me with the tools. We should stop looking to the United States as a solution to our carceral problems and actually start looking at countries that are making life better and closing down prisons, and have better social security to help the population.

Kevin Walby: Thank you, Wendy. Thank you so much for making those comments on a vision for real safety, and no longer relying on incarceration and fostering the harm that it does in our world. Okay, we're going now on the same question to Lindsay.

Lindsay Jennings: Thanks, Kevin. I think that if we were to look back at all these different webinars from the past few years, a lot of the things the key supports that everybody is highlighting are the same key supports that we've been asking for decades.

I want to speak to Ontario because we need a political culture shift. I don't necessarily call it support. We went through the pandemic with Sylvia Jones as our Solicitor General and, to her, corrections were doing everything great. That was her only comment. Our new Solicitor General hasn't even made any public acknowledgement or comment since seeing the conditions inside our jails in our province. Sylvia Jones didn't address the deaths. Michael Kerzner currently isn't addressing the deaths inside.

As an advocate, I think funders need to start funding more grassroots and peer-led organizations. We can learn from some of the other provinces. With Chantel out east, there's more development and there's more movement in a better direction, but here in Ontario, our governments don't care and it's very obvious. I don't know how to answer your question, honestly. I think that in Ontario we need to figure out how to convince people that incarcerated folks are human beings, that we're not just cast aside, we shouldn't be cast aside. The government just ignores the call-outs. The government ignored thousands of emails, calls, open letters, rallies, class actions – what more? We've had expert panels. We've had reports. We have data, we have everything you've asked for decades, and nobody says anything.

For me, specifically in Ontario, our voter turnout is important. I don't want to turn it into politics, but I guess that's kind of where I'm stuck when

I'm looking at deaths in custody. I'm surrounded by death all the time. Families just want some closure and answers about their loved ones. It's about bureaucracy and it's politics. Ontario's in a really shitty situation. We need to start voting. We need to. We need to trust our government again here in Ontario. There are so many people that are impacted by criminalization and incarceration. Whether you've been inside or you're supporting somebody inside or you're working in this sector, you know?

I'm not trying to be rude and call out, but we really need numbers right now. People going to jail right now are dying at alarming and fast rates. We need a definite change and we need more numbers. We need support from the activists, the people with lived experience, grassroots organizations, the ones that are trying to do this work and trying to address programming inside, trying to get housing for people to come out on bail. We're trying to get all the support in place. We just need funding and we need people to believe in us, and to believe that the folks inside need support and that incarcerated human beings deserve their human rights. We just need pressure from everybody who's either on this call or doing this work across, at least, Ontario. We need support and we need numbers, and a new government.

Kevin Walby: Thank you, Lindsay. Thanks for bringing up the broader parameters of struggle around this issue and the need for cross-movement, solidarity, and building bridges. Next, we're going to go back to Deepan.

Deepan Budlakoti: I actually agree with Lindsay on all her points. There's nothing really much more for me to say because she pretty much covered everything. I say that bail should be looked at as it's looked at in different provinces. In Ontario, it's extremely hard to get bail. You could be found not guilty and have done more time if you go to trial and go through the whole process than actually being released in society. Essentially, the provisions in place in Ontario, where on one hand on the *Charter* states that you're innocent until proven guilty and, on the other, you're denied for various reasons.

I think that there should be an overhaul of bail and everyone should be granted bail instead of doing time in a detention centre. That's essentially violating your constitutional rights at multiple levels, as well as not abiding by international obligations or Mandala Rules. I believe that bail itself should be looked at in Ontario, where individuals are being released on whatever conditions may be. The system is broken, and you're not helping anyone by detaining an individual for long periods of time. You affect their mental health, you affect their bodily functions in terms of eating properly, and you affect their ability to stay in contact with family and employment.

I want emphasize that everything Lindsay is saying, I 100 percent support. Though, in the interim, there should be an overhaul in regard to bail so that people don't spend a ridiculous amount of time incarcerated. The whole process itself is preposterous and deeply flawed. Those are my submissions. Thank you.

Kevin Walby: Thank you, Deepan. Thank you so much for those insights and a real concrete step that could be taken right away. Next, we're going to go to the same question to Christophe.

Christophe Lewis: Where do I even chime in? I feel like everybody covered every single ground I would want to cover, but there's always more, so I'll delve into some things. I think the consensus amongst everybody would be programming and funding. That's definitely of the most importance. I think there needs to be more programs for mental health. It's difficult for me even to find a therapist as a partially-free person. Even though I have been granted full parole, you don't feel free once you have this stigma of a life sentence hanging over your head. You never really feel completely free, so I'll put that out there just for those that don't understand. I do think mental health support is something that's definitely a need in our communities. I can benefit from using a CSC psychologist or therapist.

When you utilize the system for their services, they basically are in control of all of that information, and they can utilize that information against you moving forward so it can affect you when you're going in front of the parole board. You don't have the same rights as a regular person. It's costly to hire a therapist – even $100 an hour. Not only that, but also finding one that I could identify with because that's a big thing too. You can find a therapist and you can identify with them. There needs to be a lot of funds delegated to different communities and a more diverse background of people, so that people of those diverse backgrounds can benefit from having therapists. That's something I could speak on from my personal experience. Even at my university that I go to, I tried to go through therapy there and I wasn't able to find someone I could identify with.

Mental health support is one. Employment-specific initiatives is another one. I really think need we need to focus because for me coming out with a criminal record like mine, it's very difficult. There's so much I can go into like this is just the ID that I was released with [holds up a picture of his identification]. That's all I had, and I tell people this when I do workshops and seminars. I was released with no ID. I was released with just that CSC-issued card because I wasn't being supported for my day parole. They said, "well, we don't have to support you getting your identification because we're not supporting you for parole. We don't believe that you're going to get it".

Long story short: I got parole and showed them that even regardless of you guys not supporting me, I still got it. But now what am I going to do? I'm only being released with this identification. Imagine having to go to a federal building and presenting this to them or applying for a job and presenting this to them. When I was released amid COVID, trying to go get my vaccine was another thing. I was coerced into getting my shots, which is an issue that I know is contentious for everyone. I'm not going to really get into all that, but if I didn't take my shots I would have been labelled as a non-conformist. I was compelled to take the shots, but even when I did, I couldn't even go and get my vaccine passport because all I had was this [holds up ID again], so I had to jump through many hoops to be able to get identification.

There needs to be programs that are geared towards making sure rules are followed. They can't just be people that are in cahoots with the system. You can't have another correctional officer looking over another correctional officer. It just doesn't work, they're colleagues. They're in cahoots with each other. Obviously, they're going to rule in favour of their colleague. People from prisons transitioning to society need to have more help in terms of getting employment because if they can't be employed, what do you think they're going do? They're going to resort back to what they originally did.

During COVID, all this stuff was exacerbated. You couldn't go into certain places without proper identification. You had to book online and a lot of people don't even know how to deal with computers. Even certain social media I had to learn over. There needs to be programs that teach people soft and hard skills to be able to help them in their transition, and learning more about specific trades.

There's so much I could talk about and I know that we're limited on time. I'll just say that there are many organizations that say that they support prisoners and they won't even hire a prisoner that has lived experience.

There needs to be more accountability for those people as well. To be honest, for those reasons but not limited to those reasons, I felt the urgent need to found and register my own non-profit organization, the Freedom is a Must Foundation. I really felt the need to do that because there isn't a lot of support for people with lived experience.

I thank you guys for bringing all of us together with our lived experiences to share and talk about the issues that affected us while inside, and now that we're in the community it's really important. And I thank you guys for having me. And freedom is a must. And just always remember that broken crayons can still colour because, even though we have been broken and bent, we can still make something of ourselves.

Kevin Walby: Thank you, Christophe, for all those insights and points about things that can be changed right away and that people with lived experience have a lot of insights too. On with the same question, we're going to turn to Patricia.

Patricia Whyte: I think everybody's on the same page. There are some amazing advocates on this panel. I'm so honoured to be sitting with everyone. I do want to say that I'm a firm believer in safer communities and a die-hard abolitionist. I believe in supportive housing. I do want to piggyback off what Christophe was saying about people with lived experience – at the Elizabeth Fry Society, we just opened a thrift store that employs all of the women that we support. I hate calling them "clients" because it's kind of like a power thing for me and I don't like that since I was a client with Elizabeth Fry before. We teach them employment skills, and provide them supportive living and housing. We pay the people that live there to clean and provide peer support.

It's super important because you have to remember, individuality is huge. Everybody is different. We have to think of harm reduction and the "why?" Why are they going through what they're going through? Is it mental illness? Is it an addiction? Is it abuse and trauma? Everybody's story is different and we need to remember that. Even for myself, as an Indigenous person, I got out to a white halfway house with a white parole officer and program facilitator, and I felt no connection with anybody until I found my own wrap-around support in the community and built it for myself. What happens to the women and the men that can't do that? They slip through the cracks and they go back to prison where they're comfortable. That's why the majority of Indigenous women want to stay because they have access to their medicines, sweats, and an Elder. When they get out here, they have nothing.

CSC owns the people that are on parole. They make them go to their dentist and psychologist. What if they don't fit and have that connection? Why can't it be about what the individual person needs? Everybody's story is different. Everybody's path is different. Thankfully, I work for an organization that prides itself on employing people who have lived experience because who can do it better than someone with lived experience? You're not going to connect with somebody that doesn't know what you're talking about or hasn't walked a similar road as you. We do pride ourselves on that. We do have two amazing supportive living houses. We have a 10-bedroom six-plex for Indigenous women. Each unit is subsidized. $570 for a two-bedroom, everything is included and pet-friendly. Sometimes they have a criminal record and can't get into housing. Instead, they have to live in the hood, which is a high-risk situation for some people. Individuality and treating people like equals is our number one mandate.

I want to thank everybody today. Listening to you all, I'm very grateful. Thank you again, Kevin and Justin. You guys are amazing. Thank you for the invite.

Kevin Walby: Thank you, Patricia, for all those comments and for the work that you're doing to help people survive.

Patricia Whyte: Thank you, Kevin, very much.

Kevin Walby: And on this question, we have the last speaker, Sara.

Sara Tessier: Thank you, Kevin. I mentioned earlier about the JEC Project, and I think it's important just to mention how we can change things for the future. In May 2020, just weeks after the COVID-19 pandemic hit the Province of Nova Scotia, when the Premier declared a state of emergency, three community non-profit organizations came together: the John Howard Society of Nova Scotia, which focuses on support for men experiencing criminalization; the Elizabeth Fry Society in mainland Nova Scotia; and Coverdale Courtwork Society, both of which serve women, trans, and non-binary people experiencing criminalization to respond to the urgent needs of provincially incarcerated people.

From the 1st of May to the 13th of September 2020, JEC supported people who were leaving jail and also experiencing homelessness, ensuring a positive reintegration experience by providing release planning, justice system advocacy, and shelter with appropriate support. This needed a unique window of opportunity to support as many jail releases as possible, while also demonstrating the possibility of decarceration more broadly, and advocating for more effective and responsible reintegration pathways.

Prior to spring 2020, Nova Scotia didn't have any adequate processes in place to properly support community reintegration for people exiting incarceration. The province had one of the highest rates of remand in the country and the provincial jail already over-relied on local homelessness. In the context of the pandemic, shelters for individuals released from incarceration were operating at a reduced capacity and completely full or other housing options were eliminated. The extraordinary leadership and collaborative efforts that followed resulted in the greatest remand reduction effort in the history of the province, with a nearly 50 percent decrease in the provincial prisoner population.

During the first wave of COVID-19, over a few short days in March 2020, the provincial court, under the direction of Chief Judge Pamela Williams, heard every non-contested bail application brought forward by the crown and defence. The court supported bail plans for over 100 people facing charges. Corrections, staff court workers, lawyers, and community agencies worked vigilantly to develop appropriate release plans to assist people with reintegration. In the first weekend of this effort, more than 40 people were released from remand on bail. They applied lens of harm reduction informed feminist and anti-oppressive theories and practices. Each of these theories and practices is interconnected, and we're an integral part of that model.

Now by June 13th, 2020, the Affordable Housing Association of Nova Scotia's funding was completely depleted and, for the remaining three months of JEC, the United Way provided funding to continue. That said, with less funding the scope of the project shifted, including not having staff at either of the hotels. Staff began working at the Coverdale office. They limited onsite support. The workers for JEC would often find out the day of that the guests had to check out and they were left scrambling with the guests to either keep them in the hotel or move them to a homeless shelter or elsewhere.

Other problems began to rise. Without notice, the direction changed. We lost operational funding and the Department of Community Services moved to a model where they directly funded clients to reside in hotels without the support of JEC staff. Community services also require clients to contact shelters as soon as possible. If the shelter bed became available, they had to take it and check out of the hotel, and this created distress as guests would often be forced to leave what had been their home for many weeks. In some cases, the alternative would be sleeping outside or reincarceration, depending on the court conditions. This also caused problems for clients who were on house arrest as they needed to have court approval to move locations, and we began to see more and more breaches of court-ordered conditions and reincarceration. When the funding was secure in the beginning months, we saw very few breaches or recidivism. The chaotic change created a great deal of uncertainty and forced people back into survival mode.

The majority of the JEC guests were on bail and awaiting trial. Due to the pandemic, many court services were delayed and this extended the time for which people would be under restrictions imposed by the courts. The JEC Project allowed individuals to have a safe space to live, while determining the next steps. Some individuals who access services didn't come directly from provincial or federal jails, but many have had histories of criminalization or poverty that have created barriers to finding stability. The JEC Project was able to provide space for those individuals to live at the hotels and access support to mitigate recidivism and provide resources and tools to move forward in a safe and positive way.

In the fall of 2020, just five months following its launch, the JEC Project ran out, which meant the three agencies parted ways and the project staff were deployed back to their positions. In the end, many JEC clients returned to jail. In February 2021, Coverdale Courtwork Society, led by Ashley Avery, sought and received funding from the Affordable Housing Association of Nova Scotia to run a six-month pilot project called Caitlan's Place, a house for women and gender-diverse individuals. They had supervision and support, and reintroduced services aimed at reducing rates of remand in the province, and break harmful cycles of incarceration and homelessness. In Nova Scotia, it's not uncommon for women to be released from jail to homelessness, which seals the fate of some of our most marginalized and vulnerable community members. Caitlan's Place stepped up to address this critical need and become part of the fabric of the central services located in the Halifax region. As pilot funding ran out, Coverdale was very fortunate. I was able to step in as part of the Northpine

Foundation and commit to funding the project, which allowed it to continue and permitted the expansion from four bedrooms to 18 bedrooms and the increased number of clients would go from six to 15.

We also assisted with start-up costs, professional development and training research development for staff, employment support, education, peer support, and recreational programs. The staffing model was increased from one to two staff on-site with a house director, as well as a comprehensive team of interdisciplinary professionals. I reached out to Ashley Avery at the beginning and said, "who do you need in the community that we can support to help you?" We can build this learning ecosystem. We also funded Black Power Hour, Shelter Nova Scotia, Stepping Stone Nova Scotia, and The North End Recreation Centre. All these community organizations were an integral part of the success.

Since opening the doors, 71 women have called Caitlan's Place home. According to the data collected, between September 1st, 2021 and June 17th, 2022, just three women were released from a correctional facility to a homeless shelter. However, between January 1st, 2020 and September 10th, 2020, 75 women were released from a correctional facility to a homeless shelter. It's evident that Caitlan's Place is successfully interrupting the homelessness cycle by offering supportive housing targeted to the needs of this population. By funding this, we were able to prove this model of success and actually reached out to the Department of Community Services, which now permanently provides operational funding.

We always talk about how criminalization is so underinvested, but it's not. It's one of the most overinvested areas. It's just invested in the wrong areas. We're investing it in the punitive areas. What we need to do is reallocate those funds and put them into community-based organizations. The organizations that are doing this work and that's a big part of my job at Northpine. I'm trying to change the way philanthropy works, the way government works, and the way any traditional funding works. And now, Caitlan's Place actually just invested again to develop a new program, which will support people who are ready for recovery as opposed to harm reduction practices. It's a safe place and that again will be supported by the Department of Community Services. We need to change the way people fund. We need to change the way government puts its money into the broad areas. And we need to change the way everything is done. So it's a lot of work, but we'll get there.

CONCLUSION

Kevin Walby: Thank you, Sara. Thank you for that example. That really concrete example of the work that you're doing, and the dedication and devotion that you have for this work. If there's anyone in the audience with questions for the panellists, you can email them to me (k.walby@uwinnipeg. ca) or Justin (justin.piche@uottawa.ca). I just want to thank everyone in the audience for attending.

It's clear from what we've heard today, the COVID-19 pandemic has really exacerbated the harms and challenges faced by criminalized people in ways that actually undermine our health, well-being, and safety. We need to move beyond the prison pandemic. We need to divert and decarcerate people from custody, and we need to build communities, not cages, to meet the needs of all people, prevent violence, and then respond to it in transformative ways when we can, and also ensure that those who are behind bars for the time being are treated in a more humane and dignified manner to the extent that one can be while incarcerated in a site of confinement.

Thanks to all of our expert speakers for your brilliant and beautiful perspectives and voices, and for all the work that you do. Thanks to Caroline Faucher from the Human Rights Research and Education Centre for all the work that you did to make this webinar possible, and thanks to our ASL interpreters, Tanya and Heather, for the work that you did to make this event more accessible.

Do visit the CPEP website (www.cp-ep.org) and you will see in the days ahead that this webinar will be available there as a video, and a segment in the *Journal of Prisoners on Prisons*. Take care and stay safe, I'll pass it over to Justin.

Justin Piché: Thanks to you all for painting a picture of the changes we need to build safer communities for everyone. Let's continue the dialogue on how we can move beyond the prison pandemic.

ABOUT THE PRISON PANDEMIC PARTNERSHIP

The Centre for Access to Information and Justice (CAIJ), the Criminalization and Punishment Education Project (CPEP), and the Canadian Civil Liberties Association (CCLA) came together as the Prison Pandemic Partnership to examine the impact of COVID-19 on jails, prisons, and penitentiaries across the country. From December 2020 to April 2023, this initiative was funded through a Social Sciences and Humanities Research Council of Canada Partnership Engage Grant (1008-2020-0238) led by Kevin Walby (principal investigator) of the University of Winnipeg, Justin Piché (co-investigator) of the University of Ottawa, and Abby Deshman (partner) in her previous role at the CCLA prior to returning to private practice as a lawyer with St. Lawrence Barristers.

CONTACT

Prison Pandemic Partnership
c/o Kevin Walby, PhD
University of Winnipeg
515 Portage Avenue
Winnipeg, Manitoba, Canada
R3B 2E9

k.walby@uwinnipeg.ca

PRISONERS' STRUGGLES

Agenda: Broken Corrections
Ken (Salamander) Hammond

I am a prisoner in the care of Correctional Services of Canada (CSC) and have been incarcerated for around a quarter century. I have to ask all government parties, when is corrections going to be a priority on the country's agenda? In the past many years, it has become apparent that the federal penitentiary system is broken and it is time to fix it.

What is CSC and whom does it adhere to? Is it the public? Is it the weak and disadvantaged? What is it meant for and how are its goals achieved? I have the privilege of saying to the public that CSC is a broken branch of the government and is no longer a public service. It has blossomed into a entity run like a business by the culprits responsible for your taxes being changed into a commodity.

What is CSC's purpose? Is it rehabilitation? Is it incapacitation? Can anyone determine what the functions of corrections are? If so, it is time for all political parties to look into what it is and how the tax dollars of the Canadian people are being spent. Is the public ready to hear the truth about whose pockets are being filled?

As a prisoner, I need to first off relay to the general public is that rehabilitation is not offered here in Correctional Services of Canada, specifically in Mission Institution as a whole, including both medium and minimum facilities. Rehabilitation is something that a prisoner has to pursue on their own accord and grasp on their own terms.

Let me introduce myself. I am a Native American prisoner sentenced to a term of 20 years-to-life for second degree murder. I have no sex offences and no drug offences. I am an American citizen awaiting deportation to the United States.

I have completed every program that I was allowed to take. I say that because I cannot take the sex offender program as I am not a sex offender. I did apply to do the drug program but that only lasted a day because it was discovered that I was not into the drug scene and was not involved in a drug related incident. I was removed because it was not required for me to take such a program. I wanted to take the program just to learn something, but I was denied. I have never been drunk in my life and that is, thankfully, to the environment in which I grew up. I have taken many courses and gained many learning tools to help occupy my mind to learn and grow as a person. I have also learned that somewhere in a sentence, I had to grow up and take responsibility for my crime and do something about it.

What did I do? It took a while, but I finally grew up and realized that I can sit pouting, simmer in anger, and wallow in my own self-pity, or I can put aside that negative mindset and do something productive with my time. Let me just say, I am no angel, and I have a past in the United States. Upon completion of my sentence, I was/am supposed to be deported to California, as I have a warrant out for parole violation there.

In my years in prison, I have completed my correctional plan, did the Integrated Correctional Program Model (ICPM) maintenance three times and was told I needed some improvement (life lesson). I also completed many other programs and university courses. I am self-taught in the craft of plumbing since no one was around to teach me so I took it upon myself to read and learn it anyway because it is something I enjoy. I was told that I never learned anything. Does this writer seem to be unintelligent to you? Life living needs some improvement every day in our society.

I have been in Mission medium facility for almost a decade and I have noticed something more and more: no one is getting released and no one is really moving on to minimum or really anywhere for that matter. The programs that are offered are also not helping in anyway, except that it is money allotted to use on a reason to cover someone's ass.

The Parole Board of Canada and the parole system more broadly is broken. It is set up for one thing only and that is failure. A prisoner should not be sent back to prison because of how they dress or if they are having a bad hair day, or for just not looking right in the eyes of a parole officer. Unless the person is committing a crime, they should not be sent back. It is one thing to be drunk or something like that, but it is another to just be a few minutes late to a halfway house because someone said something that is untrue. There has to be something in place to protect the individual as a person with their act together.

It is increasingly difficult to get jobs nowadays. For the establishment to keep violating criminalized people and sending them back to prison because it can is not at all reflective of an institute that is rehabilitative in nature. Rather, it is punitive in nature and to show I know what I am talking about, if anyone can do a survey on CSC, you will notice that from roughly

September/October every year, the incarcerated/returned are at a higher rate as it is funding time, and the release rate is high during the months of April/May once the annual budget is approved.

CSC fills the beds in the fall, particularly before they must submit the budget for the following March, as they get funding for filling all the beds with prisoners. Parole violators are the simplest to incarcerate and easier to justify as there is no official oversight body that really looks in that direction. No one is watching.

The following spring prisoners are then released and all that money meant to fulfill its duties of accommodating the prisoners is allocated somewhere else, as there is now no one in the beds. Staff members can instead have a new desk or computer in their office or nice chairs. Either way, the funding is spent on something for a staff member to enjoy, while prisoners are left to survive on their own.

The meal system is the same. The cook-chill program was invented for someone to find a way to embezzle money from the public and give prisoners the least amount of nourishing sustenance possible. In doing so, it has become obvious that what was meant to be a money saving business turned into a lucrative money maker for corporations in the culinary business. The meals are now the least tasteful that they have ever been. The cook-chill program took a good quality learning opportunity from those whom would have benefitted from actually learning the culinary arts. Just because a prisoners may not be learning in the actual classroom does not mean they are not allowed to or unable to learn a trade by taking it upon themselves to study and learn the craft. It provided a chance to take up their own initiative and make themselves feel like they had accomplished something on their own.

I am not bashing CSC. I am just stating factual issues that have been ignored for far too long. It is time for the Canadian government to step up and make the necessary changes. Former Prime Minister Stephen Harper's roadmap is still the compass directing our road today when it comes to corrections and I believe it is the wrong road for our industrialized society of today to follow.

What is rehabilitation? What is required of a prisoner to be declared in that status of recovery? There is no such status as rehabilitation is not a recognized function of corrections, as those released by either the Parole Board of Canada or on statutory release are more likely to be returned to prison, as this system has created a revolving commodity. Corrections is no longer a viable institution of corrective measures and has grown into a branch of the Canadian government whose jurisdiction is in justification.

From my vantage point, it is not about releasing prisoners who are the most likely to never return. It is about identifying who we think we can release, assured that they will return and thus keep the business going. How we can justify their return and allow our employees to be driving the best cars or having the best equipment in our arsenal, thus not encouraging prisoners to be productive members of a community near you. We want them returned.

This is not an assumption. This is factual data and needs to be looked into by the community watchdogs, as CSC more often than not does not listen to the Office of the Correctional Investigator. I actually believe some of the investigators themselves like the fact that they get a free paid trip to beautiful British Colombia. They are not actual watchdogs as they get their piece of the pie too. In my years of incarceration, I have seen that no one knows what is happening inside the prisons they are running, no one knows what the other department is doing, and certainly no one is accountable within the institutions funded by the Canadian government.

Today, CSC is a broken branch of the Government of Canada that cannot be fixed and needs to be rebuilt from the ground up. Please keep in mind again that, although it may seem like I am bashing the CSC, this is not my intention. I am not the most literate prisoner, but I do have the mentality of a convict. My honour is my word, about which I am being truthful.

Attacking a prisoner with mentally abusive behaviour is not the way correctional services of today is supposed to be functioning. As a prisoner, I am supposed to recognize why I am here, repent, and grow into a law abiding individual who upholds community morals and ideologies. This is not something I was taught. It was something I took from my own personal beliefs to bring about a proper change within myself and did something to see to it that I grew up within the parameters of what is expected.

I am 60 years old now. I am an old man with nothing to look forward to in my future but death – that is how I feel and it is a reality that I have to accept. I have done more than expected in order to not only repent for having taken a life, but I also opened doors to allow me to prevent others from doing the same kind of damage I have done.

The world has changed, the prisoners have changed, and CSC has waned into complete ignorance of what should be today in yesterday's society.

I have done my own research into accountability and mentally abusive behaviour. I came to realize that my captors are supposed to emulate positive behaviour and teach prisoners how to return into communities as responsible adult individuals, and boy, is society not in for a surprise.

These kids have come into the system and they have no idea of what it is they are supposed to learn, considering that is all they talk about is feelings in programs, but they also need to learn skills in order to be productive members of today's society. The only thing they are learning is to bully and take for their own survival, and it has blossomed out into communities near you. We are not talking about repentant individuals, rather we are talking about the individuals who take programs because just it is what they need to get out, so they can get their next fix, brag about why they were incarcerated or whom they victimized.

CSC has failed to come to terms that society today has expanded its expectations of what it is expected to achieve in its facilities. They have ignored those whom have demonstrated in actuality the changes that I am sure most of Canadian society would love to see for incarcerated individuals.

What have today's prisoners learned in today's prisons? I have seen rehabilitation go ass backwards. I seem to stay out of trouble. Please remember, I am in a prison. Treat it like a war zone with a kill or be killed attitude. Sometimes, even at my age, every few years I have to step up and fight some stupid kid, as they seem to think they can bully me or someone of either a small stature or of old age. It seems to be that those who are an average age of 30 years or younger behave this way more often, while those who are of 50 years plus are the least problematic.

If a prisoner is doing good or staying out of trouble, they are treated as if they must be up to no good, and are punished more so than say a guy caught with a needle in his arm and a cellphone. Corrections has taught prisoners such as myself that no matter what actually happened, if a staff member says you did something, whether or not it is actually true, it becomes truth. It is not about guilt or innocence, it is about probability. It is often assumed that prisoners are always the ones trying to manipulate or fabricate, but it happens more so amongst the staff of Correctional Services of Canada. Somehow, opinions turn into facts and there is nothing a prisoner can do to contest the fabrications, because fiction has become fact in the eyes of Correctional Service of Canada. They tell us to be accountable for our actions and, when you are, you are neither sincere enough or do not show enough empathy or remorse. However, sadly, some of us were just taught to hold those feelings deep inside, as we too were once a victim of some priest or counsellor. To hold that against us is another story all together.

I am Native American. I too was taken from my home in the United States. I too was in our own form of residential schools. I too was abused and forgotten and thrown away to the wolves. I too was taught many things that I am told is wrong in today's society, yet I am a product of what my government wanted me to be.

I was taken from my home at five years old. My mother tried to kill herself and I was placed in a home for kids in Skillman, New Jersey while my mother was across the street in the mental hospital. We were allowed a supervised visit once a week. My mother and I ate the same food, as it was trucked over from the mental hospital to the home for kids.

I was beaten and molested many times by either a priest or counsellor. I need someone to keep in mind that corrections said I was a problem child, that I was being bad. This is stated in the reports and my reply is how much trouble could I have possibly been at the tender age of five years old. I just lost my whole family, including my beloved mother, in one scoop and it was apparently my fault, as a child, that I was emotionally torn apart and had no idea what was going on or what had really happened.

I am to blame, they say. How shameful of CSC to write such a report and use it to retain me further in their system. I say to you, Joe Public, I only became criminal because I was forced to learn to rely on my survival instinct and use it to protect myself.

I am told by the Parole Board of Canada that the empathy and emotions expressed in my explanations are an insufficient farce. Apparently, I did not show enough empathy or emotions. I remember two priests punishing me for some reason when I was 10 years old, forcing me to pluck thorn bushes with my bare hands. I only remember the pain and my bloody hands, but I endured and shed no tears. It was just before that incident that I decided I would no longer show them any emotion. I would not give them the satisfaction.

For a period of time just before the thorn bush experience, I was being molested at least once a week by a counsellor. I reported it to someone and all they did was call in the counsellor who, of course, denied it. The molesting not only continued, but became more frequent.

Am I sorry if I am a bit bitter and learned how to withhold any feelings or emotions? Am I wrong, a liar, and at fault? I was in a visit with an ex-wife once, and a guard was walking in the direction of our table. Even though I really was not doing anything wrong or illegal, I felt guilty just because I had been conditioned to feel that way. My wife pointed out the look on my face, and I felt so ashamed and defeated. Bitterness is not who I am. What I have done is I matured and grown up. I follow the culture and hold it close to my heart – it is because of my culture that I am still here today. There were many times in the past that I wanted to just fade away and die.

I have been in Mission medium for over nine years and I have been approached twice by new institutional parole officers saying, "Oh, we have to try to get you to minimum security". They come back a few days later only to say, "Sorry, there is nothing we can do for you".

I actually applied for access to Medical Assistance in Dying. CSC has dangled a carrot in front of me for a quarter century, and I am mentally and emotionally exhausted. During my last parole hearing, I told the Parole Board of Canada that if there is no hope for me and I am never getting out of prison, I would respect it so much more if someone would tell me upfront. At the end of my hearing, after the recorder was turned off, one member told me I can read between the lines to answer my question. That is when I actually gave up trying to get out, and now I accept and pray for my death to happen sooner rather than later.

I have put in for a transfer to Beavercreek medium (Fenbrook) and I am accepted. I am still, however, looking at considering medically assisted dying in the future. My only purpose, as I write these words, is to die in prison and, as such, I now believe the only dignity I have left is in choosing when and how I will die in here.

So, for those who never wonder what happens on the inside with regard to CSC, I can tell you that it has further destroyed every emotion I ever tried to experience. CSC penitentiaries are residential schools, just hidden by a different name, but operating with same purpose and perpetuating the same discrimination and violent actions against people. It has been established that those of us at Mission Institution were hit hardest by the COVID-19 outbreak and the pandemic continues to be running this place. Almost two years later, we are still feeling the effect. I have mentioned, I am Native American and I am also a Pipe Carrier.

On 5 May 2020, my cell door was opened and the Indigenous Liaison Officer stood in the doorway to say, "Sorry, Mr. Hammond, your sister passed away", and then closed the door. It happened so fast that it took me a few minutes to grasp what he had said. So I had to bang on my door and, when he returned, I had to ask "which sister". He did not know. It took me four days to find out which sister of mine had passed away and that she had died due to COVID-19 in New Jersey. We were in complete isolation ourselves and had been since 2 April 2020. There are still modifications to operations in effect to this day. Anyway, I figured since I am a Pipe Carrier and isolated, there should be no reason for me not to conduct a pipe ceremony in my cell.

I had placed many requests beforehand. I was told that now was not the time to do a pipe ceremony and no one wanted to give me tobacco. It was a full year later that I conducted such a ceremony. I filed a civil suit because I was denied access to the spiritual practices of my culture, and yet the Catholic Chaplin can take his followers into the chapel by cohort.

What has transpired in the past has left me spiritually broken until this very day. The only hope I had was with a lawyer, Julia Riddle, and she allowed me to be human again and helped in preparing a lawsuit, but today it is a waiting game. So, to say I have no emotions or empathy, or that I am not human, why allow me to live if you only expect me to die?

It is a fact that CSC is broken. Does this writer seem unbalanced or untrue? I am just a human being, treated without any dignity or extended any empathy. I am an incarcerated commodity. Slavery was supposed to have been outlawed, but prisons are instead a hidden residential school for those who the government wants to hide. CSC gets paid for hiding what its actual purpose is. They are pulling authoritarian stunts and getting away with it.

Look, I can ramble and I could point fingers, but I take responsibility for my actions. I take responsibility for taking a life. I take responsibility for hurting many families and my community as a whole. I offer my life and accept why CSC will not allow me to be accountable. What does it matter? I give my life and it is over.

Rehabilitation is a figment of our imagination that no longer has a place in the process of corrections. Corrections is broken and a complete failure. It is no longer a viable branch of the Government of Canada. It is time to rebuild it from the ground up and take a stance, as former prisoners are coming to communities near you in the future and a number of them have nothing but confusion on their minds.

ABOUT THE AUTHOR

Ken Hammond is currently imprisoned at Mission Medium Facility. He can be reached at the following address:

Ken Hammond
Mission Medium Facility
P.O. Box 60
Mission, BC
V2V 4L8

Natural Life
Steven King Ainsworth

I am a poor white man, with over 55 years behind bars in various types of confinement facilities, including U.S. Army stockades, a Marine Corps brig, city and county jails, as well as California state prisons. In May of 2020, I celebrated the 43rd anniversary of my ongoing incarceration. During that span, I have spent 22 years on Death Row at San Quentin, 11 years at California State Prison-Sacramento (New Folsom), and the last nine years here at R.J. Donovan Correctional Facility. I am not a convicted third striker, but I have served two prior prison terms in California's prison system.

In 1998, my death sentence was overturned. After four more years of litigation by California's top prosecutor in which the state attempted to reverse the 1998 decision, I was resentenced to a term of life without parole. I offer these experiences as my bona fides for the following positions:

- I do not believe any human being should be subject to a sentence of incarceration that exceeds the average human life span.
- No criminal sanction should result in confinement past a person's 100th birthday.
- No sentence(s) should be imposed that cause this milestone in life to be surpassed or that does not include the opportunity for rehabilitation redemption and parole.
- I do not believe in capital punishment or support life in prison without parole.[1]

I do believe that every prisoner must have hope. By that I mean a realistic hope, so that if the prisoner is able to reform themselves, make amends to those they have harmed, recognize the error of their ways, and reach the point where they are no longer a threat to themselves or others, the prisoner can hope to be released into the society with the aid, assistance, and supervision necessary to ensure public safety.

For this to happen, there must be a Board of Parole Hearings that is not subject to the whim or caprice of political pressure and is able to determine the point of optimum success in a prison term, at which time the prisoner can be safely returned to society. This is a determination that is not subject to political review (executive action) or reactive legislation based on other crimes of the moment and related public outcry. This must be a board with a mission to prioritize parole, not retention.

With the introduction of several bills to reform California's Penal Code and criminal sentencing that require a two-thirds majority vote in both the Assembly and Senate, I suggest that our representatives go whole hog and scrap the current penal code. Abolish the death penalty and do away with life without parole. In addition, repeal the three strikes law and end all enhancements and alternative sentences. If they have a two-thirds majority in favour of doing it, do it! End the piece meal approach and really start anew.[2]

I suggest and advocate for a sentence of "One Year to Natural Life" for all violent crimes with the eligibility for parole after seven years. A natural life will be defined as 100 years of life. No criminalized person will be sentenced to a term that surpasses their one 100th year of life for any single crime and/or an aggregate of crimes, no matter their age at the time that the criminal act was committed.[3]

A violent crime will be defined as an act in which a human being is physically injured or killed. All other felonies will be classified as serious or simple felonies. Although a threat of violence is not a violent crime, it is classified as a very serious crime. Serious and simple felonies will be punished with a determinate sentence of imprisonment that does not exceed the offender's 100th year of life. Such determinate terms will be based on current base terms enumerated for non-violent crimes.

There will be no enhancement of sentences now or in the future. Any alternative sentence will be permitted in lieu of imprisonment. There should be no alternative sentences that increase a term of confinement. A determinate sentence (flat time) will no longer be a free ride with automatic release. All persons convicted of non-violent offences will be subject to a public safety determination before they are released. If any offender appears to be a threat to public safety, they shall be subject to continued monitoring for a period of six months to three years with periodic review of the need to be monitored. This monitoring function will be similar in nature to a probationary period following release.

Additionally, any sentence for a simple or serious felony that exceeds seven years in itself, or in aggregate, will be subject to periodic review for possible recall of commitment and re-sentencing for purpose of early release. These periodic reviews will be conducted by a public safety committee who will also review all persons convicted of non-violent offences.[4]

To accomplish this new mode of rehabilitation and release, we must have a prison system which provides the means for all prisoners to reach the point of suitability for release. The prison system's mission must be to focus on rehabilitation rather than punishment. There will be no more warehousing of human beings. Ideally, no prison will exceed its design capacity or, better yet, house no more than one prisoner per cell.

Lastly, the policies of restitution collection must be changed. The current rate of 55 percent of any income is not only punitive, it is oppressive and extortionate, and needs to be reduced to the original setting of 22 percent at most.

With these changes to California laws and policies, the potential to regaining one's freedom will depend on a person's ability to reform themselves and prove that they are no longer a risk to public safety and are suitable for release into free society. All of these changes will be retroactively applied to all prisoners, parolees, and probationers whose sentences are impacted following the enactment of laws to accomplish these goals.

ENDNOTES

[1] In reality, life without parole is a death by imprisonment sentence. Although a sentence of life without parole and a death sentence are both subject to executive clemency, such relief is rare. Even though the current California governor has issued a blanket reprieve on executions during his term, prosecutors throughout the state are still pursuing capital punishment verdicts. The current governor has also issued more commutations of life without parole sentences than any governor since World War II. However, there remain over 5,000 prisoners in California who are still serving life without parole sentences.

[2] Most of the recent legislative actions have not been retroactive and/or contain carve outs that eliminate certain groups of offenders from the benefit of the new laws. Two outstanding exceptions to this are the youth offender parole hearing (YOPH) and the elderly parole hearings for men over 50 years old who have served 20 years. There is also an agreement in effect between the federal court and the Department of Corrections to hold parole hearings for the prisoners who have served 25 years and are 60 years of age. Both of these policies exclude life without parole condemned prisoners.

[3] In California and other jurisdictions, it has become common practice to sentence criminal defendants to multiple consecutive sentences with numerous enhancements. This practice results in criminalized people being given sentences of hundreds of years making any possibility of release way beyond a human life span.

[4] These sentences do not include a life sentence sanction and are known as "toe tag" sentences. It is expected that the prisoner will expire well before being eligible for release. At last count, there were currently at least 6,500 prisoners in California with such sentences, some of whom may qualify for both a youth offender and an elderly parole hearing.

[5] A determinate sentence is one in which the prisoner's maximum sentence is set and, in the majority of cases, they are granted time off from that sentence for good behaviour and work performed. Such a sentence is known as "flat time".

ABOUT THE AUTHOR

Steven K. Ainsworth is currently imprisoned. He can be reached at the following address:

Steven K. Ainsworth
C13201
RJDCF- D-19, 139
480 Alta Road
San Diego, CA 92179-0001
USA

Impartiality is a Fundamental and Legal Obligation of the Oklahoma Pardon and Parole Board

David Fleenor

No prisoner confined in the Oklahoma Department of Corrections has ever received a fundamentally fair and impartial clemency hearing from the Oklahoma Pardon and Parole Board. Impartiality will remain an illusion in the State of Oklahoma as long as the judiciary is permitted to appoint retired judges, district attorneys, and law enforcement to an executive board in violation of the separation of powers.

Oklahoma's Parole Board was created in 1944 by a constitutional amendment during the administration of Governor Robert S. Kerr. The Board was created as a moral policy designed to cool the passions of a citizenry that felt betrayed by former Governor Leon Philips.[1] The public was outraged when they learned that Governor Philips had granted clemency to a physician, serving a life sentence for murder, stemming from a death that was the result of an illegal abortion.[2] In an attempt to quell public unrest and restore confidence in the executive, the authors of the constitutional amendment significantly limited the clemency power of all future governors by requiring the newly created Parole Board to "impartiality investigate" and then "recommend" to the Governor only the prisoners the Board deemed worthy of clemency.[3]

At first glance, the official duties of the Board do not appear to create an irreconcilable conflict with other provisions of Oklahoma's Constitution. This is presuming, of course, that they are performed in a lawful and ethical manner. However, a closer look at the Board's composition reveals the author's corrupt intent to deny prisoners an opportunity to plead for mercy before an impartial panel and to unlawfully influence the recommendations of the Governor's appointees, to wit:

> There is hereby created a Pardon and Parole Board to be composed of five members; three to be appointed by the Governor; one by the Chief Justice of the Supreme Court; one by the Presiding Judge of the Criminal Court of Appeals.

I submit to the reader that the composition of the Board reveals an arrangement between the legislature and the judiciary to encroach upon governmental powers belonging to the executive, while appearing to act in the interest of Oklahoma citizens. I believe that the authors of the constitutional amendment turned a blind eye to the separation of powers doctrine, with the assurance from the judiciary that all legal challenges would fail, because Oklahoma prisoners do not have a liberty interest in the clemency process.[4] It is an undisputed fact that no prisoner has ever won legal decision against the Oklahoma Pardon and Parole Board – the judiciary has fiercely used its gatekeeping function to silence and keep a knee on the neck of those prisoners who dare to be heard, myself included. Furthermore, it is undisputed that the Oklahoma Pardon and the Parole Board was not created as an administrative body for the purpose of facilitating and/or ensuring public safety. Rather, it was created as a political body, by the legislature and the judiciary, both of whom agreed to limit and redistribute the powers of the executive.

On 15 September 2020, I appeared before the Oklahoma Pardon and Parole Board on an application for commutation.[5] In support of my application, I provided the Board with new evidence proving that I was factually innocent of murder in the first degree.[6] Rather than "impartially investigate" the new evidence, as required by the Oklahoma Constitution, Judge Allen C. McCall used his position on the Board to retry me using the medical evidence now proven to be false.[7] My request for clemency was denied.

On 28 April 2021, I filed a complaint against Judge McCall after discovering that he was violating the separation of powers clause. He was assigned to the Judicial Ethics Advisory Panel, while simultaneously serving as a member of the Oklahoma Parole Board.[8] My complaint was assigned to Judge Natalie Mai who, to this day, refuses to compel the court clerk to certify the summons and return it for the perfection of service. Determined to be heard, I proceeded without the summons. I served my complaint upon the Parole Board, Attorney General, and Governor with notice that the court clerk was interfering with my right to due process. On 7 July 2021, Judge McCall resigned from the Oklahoma Pardon and Parole Board.

Comprehensive changes are needed in the Board's composition before those imprisoned will ever receive a fundamentally fair and impartial clemency hearing. As a starting point, the judiciary must be separated from the executive in order to seat an unbiased panel. Impartiality of the mind cannot be achieved when uniting the powers of the executive and the judiciary in one body or person as the internal conflict between public performance and private beliefs is too great.

Publicly, Judge McCall would lead you to believe that he was a fair and impartial member of the executive by stating that "he had always tried to stand up for victims and law enforcement and give inmates a fair opportunity".[9] But privately, his allegiance to the judiciary corrupted his legal obligation of impartiality: "I absolutely trust a criminal justice system designed and refined by names like Jefferson, Adams, Jay, Madison, Marshall (John and Thurgood), O'Connor and Roberts... *So why is our Board attempting to undermine verdicts in cases of violent crimes?*"[10]

ENDNOTES

[1] Amended by State Question No. 309, Legislative Referendum No. 86, adopted at election held on July 11, 1944.

[2] "Capital Clemency in Oklahoma 1943-1966" by attorney Gary Peterson of Oklahoma City, Oklahoma.

[3] Article 6, 10 of Oklahoma's Constitution.

[4] Philips v. Williams, 608 P.2d at 1134.

[5] Oklahomadoc.zoom.us/rec/share Access Passcode: UW=Fq9SE.

[6] Affidavits from a Board Certified Neurologist; and a Board Certified Forensic Pathologist.

[7] Appointed by the Oklahoma Supreme Court.

[8] Article 7, 11 (c) of Oklahoma's Constitution.

[9] Tulsa World Newspaper.

[10] Email dated June 7, 2020.

ABOUT THE AUTHOR

David Fleenor was a 24-year-old first-time felon when 12 strangers — without any special skill or training — recommended that he spend the remainder of his natural life in prison without review after being found guilty of his first felony offense.

BOOK REVIEWS

Food as a Mechanism of Control and Resistance
in Jails and Prisons: Diets of Disrepute
by Salvador Jimenez Murguía
Lanham (MD): Lexington Books (2018) 111 pp.
Reviewed by Lucas Ridgeway

Like the plots found in literature and film, food tells a story. *Food as a Mechanism of Control and Resistance in Jails and Prisons* is a short book about food and foodways associated with the experience of serving time in jails and prisons. The stories told therein are from an academic perspective that is concerned with how the experience of food in jails and prisons can be moved beyond an item of necessity for survival into the navigation of informal economies to establish autonomy and, most importantly, as an item of both control and resistance. Taken from an examination of several international models, Salvador Jimenez Murguía offers us a vivid survey of several case studies that document how prison food is politicized as philosophies of control and resistance.

As we open and explore this hardcover edition, the reader finds that the first chapter explores how food is used as a mechanism of control. The author considers how food is manipulated to serve the interests of the correctional staff and administration and, specifically, the implications of employing food, as opposed to the use of time, in disciplinary action. Later chapters survey the quality of food in prison by taking a closer look at the qualitative attributes associated with food, inclusive of appearance, taste, nutritional values, and its distribution. Moving forward, the reader discovers chapters dedicated to how food is used as a mechanism of resistance among the incarcerated, from transforming food into products of mind alteration, weaponry, and commerce, to over-consumption for comfort, and not eating at all in protest. The final chapters detail these methods of resistance, highlighting the intended ends of innovation, survival, and pleasure respectively.

The author states that these settings of incarceration, referred to as "total institutions" (Goffman, 1961), are thus places where ordinary infractions to human rights are rampant. Like all resources within total institutions, food is vulnerable to manipulation. In a jail or prison setting, food therefore innately becomes both a mechanism of control and resistance. In the former, the type of food, its quality, its quantity, and the symbolic significance of its presence or absence all contribute to the sociopolitical experience of the incarcerated. The author surmises all this without having lived it, but attempts to do so with all humility, thus viewing food within total institutions as social facts that engender real consequences.

At the heart of this book is a concern that the least socially acceptable among us are also the most vulnerable to the misuses and abuses of power, in even the slightest of expressions. This text is primarily about the precarious situation that those with stained statuses must face when connecting with food inside jails and prisons, with the focus being predominantly in the United States. The main objective of this digest is to open a discussion about the many dimensions of food within sites of incarceration by exposing the persistent culture of mistrust between prisoners and the corporate bodies responsible for their custody and care. Murguía, a professor at Akita International University in Japan, offers us several relevant examples to expound upon in this brief manuscript that do indeed lend themselves to global implications.

I found that the force-feeding chapter was by far the most illuminating as we see reproduced writing from an incarcerated Oscar Wilde in the 1890s at a time when the British House of Lords saw food as forming part of a prisoner's punishment and set prison diets accordingly. Later, these same policies also directly affected the Suffragette movement as imprisoned women employed the use of hunger strikes, which resulted in their mass force-feeding – a practice further detailed in modern times at Guantanamo Bay despite the 1975 decree of the World Medical Association, which prohibits force-feeding when someone is of a rational mind. Moreover, in 2013, the American Medical Association reiterated the WMA Tokyo Declaration in relation to Guantanamo's practices adding that, "every competent patient has the right to refuse medical intervention, including life-sustaining interventions" (Rosenberg, 2013).

Murguía also puts a modest spotlight on the Aramark Corporation, a major American purveyor of institutional food services, who has had employees accused of sexual misconduct, unsanitary conditions, spoiled food, unauthorized menu changes, inadequate meal portions, and administering food that was unfit for human consumption. However, he mitigates these accusations by suggesting that it would be unfair to infer that the corporate body itself engaged in any of this intentionally. Certainly, some personnel may act with malice, but it might be reasonable to assume that, like prisons themselves, major civil service operations such as Aramark simply make these mistakes by attempting to accomplish too much, while still turning over a large profit margin. This was a rationale lost on one American prisoner who was served Nutraloaf daily for 19 days and lost 14 pounds, experienced vomiting, developed digestive problems including stomach pains, constipation, and painful defecation, along with an anal fissure.

In terms of becoming organized and resisting these conditions, nearly thirty thousand prisoners of the California prison system in July 2013 went on a prearranged hunger strike to call attention to the adverse effects of long-term isolation. The strike lasted sixty days and, although the number of protestors diminished substantially, there remained at least 100 prisoners at the end. The statement that this foray bridged across twenty-four state prisons and at least four out-of-state contract facilities was remarkable, especially since four rival prison gangs that would otherwise be dedicated to taking each other out coordinated it. This event provides evidence that the politicization of food as a method of resistance was a conscious and effective decision on the part of these planners.

In Canada, food in prison has been the source of many disruptions and discontent (see, for example, Brazeau, 2020). In his 46th Annual Report to Parliament, Ivan Zinger (2019), the Correctional Investigator, wrote that prisoners were subject to "inadequate per diem (less than $6.00 per day per inmate spent on food); inconsistent or substandard meal portion sizes; failure to meet Canada Food Guide requirements; excessive amount of food wastage; (and) failure to consistently follow special diet requirements". He concludes, "Cost savings and other efficiencies in the food services area are prioritized at the expense of inmate well-being" (Zinger, 2019).

A bright light can be seen in one of the most unlikely of places, San Quentin State Prison, where the T.R.U.S.T. program (Teaching Responsibility Utilizing Sociological Training) allows for convicts to pay for food from local restaurants as a reward for 'good behaviour'. Despite the definition of good behaviour being out of their control, many captives serving life sentences can raise money to fund their rehabilitation programs, contribute to community organizations, and donate a percentage to a charity of the warden's choice, while enjoying a taste of freedom.

In conclusion, *Food as a Mechanism of Control and Resistance in Jails and Prisons* shows that the everyday micro-interactions initiated by institutional management and staff toward prisoners do reveal how food becomes a mechanism of control. The reality of control lies within a debate grounded in the division between retributive versus rehabilitative models of justice. While the reality of resistance lies within a way of establishing one's autonomy, regaining one's dignity, and expressing the qualities that make one human. With these reflections in mind, this book opens new possibilities for the future research of food settings for the incarcerated and the close study of the ways in which these diets of the disrepute serve as a mechanism for control and resistance for those that work, live, and eat within them.

REFERENCES

Brazeau, Erica (2020) "Raw Vs. The Law: Our Fight for Vegetables at the Ottawa-Carleton Detention Centre", *Journal of Prisoners on Prisons*, 29(1&2): 127-129.

Goffman, Erving (1961) *Asylums: Essays on the Social Situation of Mental Patients and Other Inmates*, New York: Anchor Books.

Rosenberg, Carol (2013) "AMA opposes force feedings at Guantánamo", *Miami Herald* – April 30. Retrieved from: http://www.miamiherald.com/news/nation-world/world/americas/guantanamo/article1950859.html

Zinger, Ivan (2019) *Annual Report*, Ottawa: Office of the Correctional Investigator of Canada. Retrieved from: https://www.oci-bec.gc.ca/cnt/comm/presentations/presentationsAR-RA1819info-eng.aspx

ABOUT THE REVIEWER

Lucas Ridgeway is a Canadian federal prisoner at Bath Institution. He is the Book Clubs for Inmates Ambassador, Protestant Representative, and Alcoholic Anonymous Chairperson. He produces a weekly radio service called *Spiritual Connection* on 101.3 FM (CJAI FM in Kingston, ON). Podcasts can be downloaded at www.cjai.ca/podcast-main/SpiritualConnection/index.php. He would like to be reached by mail at the following address:

Lucas Ridgeway
P.O. Box 1500
Bath, ON
KOH 1G0

Infinite Hope: How Wrongful Conviction, Solitary Confinement, and 12 Years on Death Row Failed to Kill My Soul
by Anthony Graves
Boston: Beacon Press (2018) 224pp.
Reviewed by 377259d

Infinite Hope: How Wrongful Conviction, Solitary Confinement, and 12 Years on Death Row Failed to Kill My Soul is the tragic autobiographical account of Anthony Graves, an innocent man, convicted of a monstrous crime and his plight through the American criminal justice system. His personal harrowing tale exposed the systemic frailties of said system in a most poignant way. Once exonerated, he ultimately compiled his story in *Infinite Hope.*

On or about 3:00am on 18 August 1992 in Somerville, Texas, six people – five of which were under the age of 16 – were brutally murdered and incinerated. A shocking and unconscionable crime for any community, it demanded justice and ultimate accountability for the perpetrator(s) responsible. Within days, the badly burned father of a four-year-old victim was arrested, interrogated, and immediately identified Graves as an accomplice. Summarily arrested, Graves' 18-year, 2-month, 4-day legal odyssey/personal hell began.

Throughout his book, Graves succinctly outlined the idiosyncratic aspects of the American criminal justice system (Miranda Rights; Grand Jury System; Evidence Disclosure Motions; Jury Impanelling, Habeas Corpus Writs, etc.) and how they related to his particular case, circumstances, and eventual conviction. Chronologically and comprehensively, he skillfully guides the reader through the procedural due process of the American criminal justice system and how it specifically impacted his case far better than any civics primer or introduction to American criminal law textbook ever could. This alone made it a must read for anyone interested in the true operation of the American criminal justice system.

Even more deftly, though, he paints a guarded picture of the life and conditions in prison as an imprisoned person on death-row. However, his narration seemed to be a rather sanitized cinema-verité version and attempt geared to a particular sympathetic audience. Curiously minimized from his storytelling was the depiction of endemic prison violence. For instance, consider this glib example: "I witnessed a lot of bad things in there. Stabbings, suicide, men going totally insane, a few killings" (p. 119), and the only violent incident mentioned (an actual shocking homicide detailed on page 133) entailed barely two paragraphs. As well, most notably, the acute racist/gang/religious division/dynamics of everyday prison living amongst his fellow prisoners was conspicuously and completely non-existent in his account, other than his equally terse statement "death row necessitated alliances" (p. 132). Perhaps this glaring omission and selective memory represents Graves' personal method of coping, but it is an obvious oversight that was odd given his otherwise accurate and moving first-hand depiction of life as a prisoner.

Finally, and fortunately, for Graves, "justice" prevailed. The conservative Texas Fifth Circuit Appellate Court overturned his conviction based on "egregious prosecutorial misconduct" and ordered a new trial. Undaunted, for approximately four years (during which he remained in solitary confinement), the state prosecutors delayed the eventual adjudication of his case with yet more questionable legal wrangling and maneuvering. Ultimately freed, Graves graciously established a foundation to help prisoners who were wrongfully convicted or "over-sentenced". As he so concisely concludes in his epilogue, "my experience as a wrongfully convicted man has given me a perspective and insight few people will ever have about our criminal justice system and its need for reform" (p 189). "No doubt, this was true and his book, *Infinite Hope*, thoroughly deserves to be heartily recommended and read for those aforementioned reasons. Moreover, his advocacy for those individuals is truly admirable and adequately detailed.

While this is one man's account, it is important to note that, according to the National Registry of Exonerations (2022), 3,176 prisoners in the United States of America have been exonerated of serious crimes since 1989. They estimate that this equates to 27,200 years of lost time.

REFERENCE

National Registry of Exonerations (2022) Irvine: Newkirk Center for Science & Society – University of California Irvine | Ann Arbour: University of Michigan Law School | East Lansing: Michigan State University College of Law. Retrieved from: https://www.law.umich.edu/special/exoneration/Pages/about.aspx

ABOUT THE REVIEWER

377259d is currently imprisoned.

Rectify: The Power of Restorative Justice After Wrongful Conviction
by Lara Bazelon
Boston: Beacon Press (2018) 237 pp.
Reviewed by Victoria Morris

Informed by Lara Bazelon's experience as a public defender, as well as interviews with exonerees and violent assault survivors, *Rectify: The Power of Restorative Justice After Wrongful Conviction* explores the negative impacts of wrongful convictions in the United States. The aim is to inform the readers as to the high number of wrongful convictions, the lack of investigation and rectification of these cases, and the healing ability of restorative justice processes between those wrongfully convicted and violent assault survivors who mistakenly identified their attacker, resulting in miscarriages of justice. The book takes a descriptive approach with each chapter examining a different aspect involved in wrongful convictions (i.e. the details surrounding the investigation, the problems in the identification process, the healing power of restorative justice, and reforms to the penal system). This process is brought to life using numerous true stories of exonerees and assault survivors.

Bazelon starts with how wrongful convictions happen – namely lies, mistakes, police misconduct, prosecutorial misconduct, junk science, false confessions, and not having a defense. She discusses the flaws within the penal system regarding wrongful convictions, such as a lack of innocence projects, state officials' stubbornness to admit they were wrong, and eighteen states still not providing financial compensation for those who are wrongfully convicted. She goes into detail about reforms enacted in some jurisdictions that have allowed for wrongful convictions to be discovered and overturned, freeing people who are wrongfully convicted from prison. States vary greatly in their attention paid to wrongful conviction, with Texas (surprisingly) leading the way with policy and laws that provide funding to prevent wrongful conviction, help exonerate those who have been wrongfully convicted, and provide $80,000 to an exoneree for every year they spent in prison. In contrast, states like Pennsylvania have severely underfunded public defenders, giving poor (and often racialized) defendants an unlikely chance of walking free. Additionally, they provide no compensation for those who have been wrongfully convicted.

Although people often assume that after exoneration the freed person lives their happy ending, Bazelon illustrates the difficulties faced after being released, including practical and emotional challenges. The road to being exonerated is often long yet is becoming more common due to the increase in innocence projects and DNA evidence that contradicts eyewitness testimonies, which are shown to be inaccurate and often coerced or influenced by police.

One of the most original contributions of this book is the use of lived experiences of sexual assault survivors who played an integral part in a wrongful conviction. Their feelings of guilt and shame for wrongfully identifying their attacker can be overwhelming and can reignite difficult memories and emotions from their assaults. Bazelon concludes with stories of how some exonerees, and survivors of violent assaults have emerged to make a positive contribution to society and specifically seek to aid people in similar situations. Throughout the book, the reader is hit with emotional stories of pain, suffering, and how restorative justice has facilitated the healing process of many violent assault survivors. The book provides an in-depth and well-rounded account of wrongful convictions and includes many narratives of how restorative justice has helped both those who have been wrongfully convicted and violent assault survivors to heal after the immense pain they have endured.

Although an intriguing read, there were several junctions where I struggled with Bazelon's approach. Bazelon privileges the law as a source of knowledge production. From this perspective, law overrides other disciplinary knowledges and claims to be morally right. This legal stance is coupled with a liberal stance which seeks incremental improvements to the current carceral structure without challenging carceral spaces (Cohen, 1985; Goodman et al., 2017). Thus, the liberal legal stance assumes that the penal system will be fair and just after we use law to reduce wrongful convictions. Overall, the author seems content with how the current penal system operates, other than the number of wrongful convictions and the lack of awareness and efforts trying to reduce these cases. Additionally, she perpetuates other harmful ideologies that marginalize other populations that 'deserve' to be treated as lesser than, while those who are wrongfully convicted should be treated better. Specifically, the writer suggests the testimony of a "drug addict" (p. 22) and a "prostitute with five outstanding warrants" (p. 44) should not be trusted. She goes as far as to suggest that "in the vast majority of cases, the criminal justice system gets it right" (p. 36). In so doing, the book reifies the punitive injustice system and carceral spaces for those who are assumed to be guilty.

Consistent with restorative justice (Pavlich, 2005) and a liberal legal stance (Goodman, et al., 2017), Bazelon uses the same language of the state, such as victim/offender and guilt/innocence dichotomies. This language assumes that we can determine who is 'guilty' and 'innocent' if the legal process is fair and just. In addition, the language normalizes the use of carceral structures, such as prison, which abolitionists have decried as being demonstrably harmful, ineffective, costly, and unjust (McLeod, 2015; Mathiesen, 2006). In contrast, transformative justice operates outside the current carceral system, challenging carceral logics – such as racism and patriarchy – and transforming harmful situations to be agents of change (Piepzna-Samarasinha et al., 2020). Additionally, transformative justice does not use the penal language of the state, nor does it privilege law as an emancipatory tool.

The most valuable aspect of this book are the narratives supplied through interviews with the assault survivors and exonerees. This offers well-informed and passionate perspectives that offer convincing evidence for the healing effect of the use of restorative justice between wrongfully convicted and assault survivors. It was interesting that every exoneree readily forgave the person who contributed to their wrongful conviction. Although a wonderful storyline, it is difficult to believe that discrepant cases do not exist. Another strength of the book is the detailed illumination of the lack of awareness and effort in investigating and rectifying wrongful convictions. This appears to be a stubbornness of the state (actors) not wanting to admit to mistakes or wrongdoings.

Bazelon effectively explores the difficult experiences of those involved in wrongful convictions, explaining the history and current state of innocent projects in the United States, and exploring the power of restorative justice in wrongful convictions. However, due to the privileging of restorative justice and the law, this book uses language and assumptions that perpetuate carceral logics. Nevertheless, this book can be appreciated for the in-depth detail about the abysmal state of wrongful convictions in the United States, the healing potential of restorative justice, and the nuanced narratives that put the reader in the shoes of the survivors.

REFERENCES

Cohen, Stanley (1985) *Visions of Social Control*, Cambridge: Polity Press.

Goodman, Philip, Joshua Page and Michelle Phelps (2017) *Breaking the Pendulum: The Long Struggle Over Criminal Justice*, Oxford: Oxford University Press.

Mathiesen, Thomas (2006[1990]) *Prison on Trial*, London: Waterside Press.

McLeod, Allegra (2015) "Prison Abolition and Grounded Justice", *UCLA Law Review*, 62: 1156-1239.

Pavlich, George (2005) *Governing Paradoxes of Restorative Justice* (first edition), Oxfordshire: Routledge-Cavendish.

Piepzna-Samarasinha, Leah Lakshmi and Ejeris Dixon (eds.) (2020) *Beyond Survival: Strategies and Stories from the Transformative Justice Movement*, Oakland: AK Press.

ABOUT THE REVIEWER

Victoria Morris is a PhD Candidate (ABD) in the Department of Criminology at the University of Ottawa whose doctoral thesis examines how diversion measures are perceived by criminalized people and workers within the community re-entry sector as lessening carcerality and/or as extensions of carceral control. She is also Online Production Editor for the *Journal of Prisoners on Prisons*.

AVAILABLE TITLES AND CALL FOR BOOK REVIEWS

Journal of Prisoners on Prisons

The *Journal of Prisoners on Prisons* (*JPP*) welcomes book review submissions. Book reviews range from 800 to 1,200 words. Interested reviewers should contact the *JPP* with a request for one of the available titles (listed below). Should the book still be available, it will be mailed immediately.

For publishers: If you would like to have your new titles reviewed in the *JPP*, please send to the address below for consideration.

Book Reviews – Journal of Prisoners on Prisons

c/o Melissa Munn

Department of Sociology

Okanagan College

7000 College Way

Vernon, British Columbia, Canada

V1B 2N5

AVAILABLE TITLES

Bourgeois, Louis (ed.) (2022) *Mississippi Prison Writing*, Oxford (MS): Vox Press, 267 pages.

Boyd, Susan (2022) *Heroin: An Illustrated History*, Halifax: Fernwood, 256 pages.

Correia, David and Tyler Wall (2021) *Violent Order: Essays on the Nature of Police*, Chicago: Haymarket Books, 222 pages.

Davis, Angela Y. (2022) *Angela Davis: An Autobiography*, Chicago: Haymarket Books, 420 pages.

Hill, Marc Lamont (2020) *We Still Here: Pandemic, Policing, Protest, and Possibility*, Chicago: Haymarket Books, 128 pages.

House, Jordan and Asaf Rashid (2022) *Solidarity Beyond Bars: Unionizing Prison Labour*, Halifax: Fernwood, 180 pages.

Jones, El (2022) *Abolitionist Intimacies*, Halifax: Fernwood, 192 pages.

Meissner, Caits (2022) *The Sentences That Create Us: Crafting A Writer's Life in Prison*, Chicago: Haymarket Books, 339 pages.

Milward, David (2022) *Reconciliation and Indigenous Justice: A Search for Ways Forward*, Halifax: Fernwood, 240 pages.

Paynter, Martha (2022) *Abortion to Abolition: Reproductive Health and Justice in Canada*, Halifax: Fernwood, 176 pages.

Reinisch, Deiter (2022) *Learning Behind Bars: How IRA Prisoners Shaped the Peace Process in Ireland*, Toronto: University of Toronto Press, 240 pages.

Wilkerson, George T. and Robert Johnson (2022) *Bone Orchard: Reflections on Life Under Sentence of Death,* Honeoye Falls (NY): Bleak House Books, 138 pages.

UPCOMING SPECIAL ISSUES – CALLS FOR PAPERS

Emotions and Carceral Spaces
Jennifer Kilty, Rachel Fayter and Justin Piché

SPECIAL ISSUE EDITORS

Jennifer M. Kilty, PhD – Professor and Chair, Department of Criminology, University of Ottawa

Rachel Fayter – PhD Candidate, Department of Criminology, University of Ottawa

Justin Piché, PhD – Associate Professor, Department of Criminology, University of Ottawa

SPECIAL ISSUE THEME

The *Journal of Prisoners on Prisons* (JPP) invites submissions for a special issue on the theme of "Emotions and Carceral Spaces". Experiences of imprisonment or living and working in various carceral settings are isolating, punitive, and at times traumatic, all of which influence the emotional experiences of both prisoners and staff. Carceral spaces are neither uniform nor orderly, and the way emotions are felt and expressed differs significantly depending on the specific setting, lived experiences, and interpersonal interactions. Different carceral environments can produce multiple emotional experiences, which can also differ based on gender, race, sexuality, and other markers of difference. Individuals' age, past experiences, length of sentence, and security level can also impact one's emotions.

We encourage authors to share and critically reflect on their emotional experiences within carceral environments or how different physical spaces in jails, prisons, treatment centres, detention centres, psychiatric facilities, halfway houses or other sites of confinement affect prisoners' moods and behaviours. Submissions that reflect how emotions are organized and expressed in prison, along with where and how it is appropriate to express oneself emotionally in the culture of prison and the policy context are especially welcomed. We hope to better understand how carceral spaces can shape people's emotional experiences, while also impacting or being impacted by interpersonal relations among prisoners, as well as between prisoners and staff.

Additionally, we invite submissions concerning how emotions contribute to prison spaces being perceived as a heightened 'HIV risk environment'. As the history of HIV/AIDS is structured by emotions such as fear, disgust, shame, and pride, we seek to foreground the lived experience of HIV-positive people to explore how they manage their emotional selves in/outside the prison and how everyday decisions in these settings are affected by an 'emotion culture' that reflects the thoughts, feelings, and perceptions of the emotional capacities of others. Thinking about carceral space as an 'HIV risk environment' can help with understanding the interplay of the physical, social, economic, and policy environments, and to consider how they affect the transmission of HIV. For example, considerations of the availability or unavailability of harm reduction measures and how the debate around these options (e.g. condoms, needle exchanges) are shaped by emotions are welcome. Through this process, we invite contributors to explore how emotions can structure harm reduction policy debates, and to better understand how emotions challenge and/or contribute to HIV risk behaviours in prison.

We welcome submissions from current and former prisoners, criminalized people, or pieces co-authored with people who have a lived experience of incarceration and allies, advocates, practitioners, and scholars from a multidisciplinary perspective. We invite submissions drawing on lived experience and/or a wide range of fields and perspectives, including but not limited to socio-legal studies, sociology, criminology, psychology, Indigenous studies, feminist and gender studies, critical race studies, queer studies, social work, philosophy, and artistic/creative interpretations of emotions and carceral spaces. Submissions from current and former prisoners who are willing to draw on their personal narratives and lived experiences to expand understanding of emotions in prison are particularly encouraged.

PAPER FORMATS

This special issue welcomes contributions from a wide range of scholarly work including:

- Auto-ethnographic accounts that examine experiences of imprisonment to illuminate broader issues faced by incarcerated people;

- Theoretical, critical and analytical essays;
- Scholarly research articles based on quantitative, qualitative, arts-based and/or mixed- methods research;
- Book reviews;
- Artistic content – photo or graphic essays, digital art, poetry, etc.;
- Interviews or discussions transcribed from recordings; or
- Commentaries.

SUBMISSION GUIDELINES

At the *JPP,* we support incarcerated people's right to exercise freedom of expression pursuant to section 2 of the *Canadian Charter of Rights and Freedoms* and embedded in national constitutions elsewhere across the world. We believe that publishing the writing of incarcerated people is a necessary tool to facilitate transparency in carceral settings. We welcome submissions from all current and former prisoners, and are eager to hear your input on the above-mentioned issues. Please share this notice with anyone who may be interested in contributing to our journal. We ask that those who choose to submit include a short biographical statement and let us know if you would like to be published anonymously. We look forward to reviewing your submissions that follow the journal's guidelines below and hope to hear from you soon.

- The Journal will not publish any subject matter that advocates hatred, sexism, racism, violence or that supports the death penalty.
- The Journal does not publish material that usually focuses on the writer's own legal case, although the use of the writer's personal experiences as an illustration of a broader topic is encouraged.
- The Journal does not usually publish fiction and does not generally publish poetry. Illustrations, drawings and paintings may be submitted as potential cover art.
- Articles should be no longer than 20 pages typed and double-spaced or legibly handwritten. Electronic submissions are gratefully received.
- Writers may elect to write anonymously or under a pseudonym.
- For references cited in an article, writers should attempt to provide the necessary bibliographic information. Refer to the references cited in past issues for examples.

- Editors look for developed pieces that address topics substantially. Manuscripts go through a preliminary reading and then are sent to review by the Editorial Board. Those that are of suitable interest are returned to the author with comments or suggestions. Editors work with writers on composition and form, and where necessary may help the author with referencing and bibliographic information, not readily available in prisons. Selected articles are returned to authors for their approval before publication. Papers not selected are returned with comments from the editor. Revised papers may be resubmitted.
- Please submit biographical and contact information, to be published alongside articles unless otherwise indicated.

IMPORTANT DATES

Submissions by authors:	1 May 2023
Editorial decision and reviewer comments to authors:	1 July 2023
Revised manuscripts:	1 October 2023
Final editorial decision to authors:	1 December 2023
Publication date:	2024

SUBMISSIONS

Via email to jpp@uottawa.ca or by mail to the address below:

Journal of Prisoners on Prisons
c/o Department of Criminology
University of Ottawa
120 University Private – Room 14049
Ottawa, Ontario, Canada
K1N 6N5

Profiling and the Canadian Carceral State |
Les profilages et l'État carcéral canadien
Justin Piché and | et Sandra Lehalle / Observatoire des profilages

SPECIAL ISSUE EDITORS |
DIRECTION DE L'ÉDITION SPÉCIALE

Justin Piché, PhD
Associate Professor | Professeur agrégé
Department of Criminology | Département de criminology
University of Ottawa | Université d'Ottawa

Sandra Lehalle, PhD
Associate Professor | Professeur agrégé
Department of Criminology | Département de criminology
University of Ottawa | Université d'Ottawa

Observatoire des profilages
www.observatoiredesprofilages.ca

SPECIAL ISSUE THEME |
THÉMATIQUE DE L'ÉDITION SPÉCIALE

The Canadian Carceral State routinely engages in profiling of people pushed to the margins by colonialism, racism and white supremacy, capitalism and classism, patriarchy and heteronormativity, ableism, and other violent structures. This is evident in who is targeted, harmed, and killed by policing, imprisonment, immigration, child apprehension, health, social services and assistance, and other carceral institutions. The *Journal of Prisoners on Prisons* invites contributions by current and former prisoners, their loved ones, and grassroots community organizations that document, critique, and propose alternatives to profiling evident in carceral practices and experiences. Prospective contributors can also submit pieces examining resistance efforts behind and beyond bars to build decarceral futures.

Les profilages des personnes marginalisées par le colonialisme, le racisme et la suprématie blanche, le capitalisme et le classisme, le patriarcat et l'hétéronormativité, le capacitisme et d'autres structures violentes est une pratique récurrente chez l'État carcéral canadien. Cela est évident lorsqu'on observe qui est ciblé, blessé et tué par les services de police, l'emprisonnement, l'immigration, l'appréhension d'enfants, de santé, ainsi que d'autres institutions carcérales. Le *Journal of Prisoners on Prisons* invite des contributions de prisonniers actuels and anciens, de leurs proches et d'organisations communautaires qui documentent, critiquent et proposent des alternatives au profilage évident dans les pratiques et expériences carcérales dont ils/elles ont vécu. Les contributeurs potentiels peuvent également soumettre des contributions portant sur les efforts de résistance derrière et au-delà des barreaux qui ont pour but de bâtir un avenir décarcéral.

CONTRIBUTION – FORMATS – CONTRIBUTIONS

This special issue welcomes contributions from a wide range of scholarly work including:

- Auto-ethnographic accounts that examine experiences of imprisonment to illuminate broader issues faced by incarcerated people;
- Theoretical, critical and analytical essays;
- Scholarly research articles based on quantitative, qualitative, arts-based and/or mixed- methods research;
- Book reviews;
- Artistic content – photo or graphic essays, digital art, poetry, etc.;
- Interviews or discussions transcribed from recordings; or
- Commentaries.

Ce numéro spécial accueille les contributions d'un large éventail de travaux universitaires, notamment:

- Récits auto-ethnographiques qui examinent les expériences d'emprisonnement pour éclairer les problèmes plus larges rencontrés par les personnes incarcérées ;
- Essais théoriques, critiques et analytiques ;
- Articles de recherche scientifique basés sur des recherches quantitatives, qualitatives, basées sur les arts et/ou utilisant des méthodes mixtes ;
- Revues de livres ;
- Contenu artistique – essais photographiques ou graphiques, art numérique, poésie, etc. ;
- Entrevues ou discussions retranscrites à partir d'enregistrements ; ou
- Commentaires.

SUBMISSION GUIDELINES |
DIRECTIVES DE SOUMISSION

At the *JPP*, we support incarcerated people's right to exercise freedom of expression pursuant to section 2 of the *Canadian Charter of Rights and Freedoms* and embedded in national constitutions elsewhere across the world. We believe that publishing the writing of incarcerated people is a necessary tool to facilitate transparency in carceral settings. We welcome submissions from all current and former prisoners, and are eager to hear your input on the above-mentioned issues. Please share this notice with anyone who may be interested in contributing to our journal. We ask that those who choose to submit include a short biographical statement and let us know if you would like to be published anonymously. We look forward to reviewing your submissions that follow the journal's guidelines below and hope to hear from you soon.

- The Journal will not publish any subject matter that advocates hatred, sexism, racism, violence or that supports the death penalty.
- The Journal does not publish material that usually focuses on the writer's own legal case, although the use of the writer's personal experiences as an illustration of a broader topic is encouraged.

- The Journal does not usually publish fiction and does not generally publish poetry. Illustrations, drawings and paintings may be submitted as potential cover art.
- Articles should be no longer than 20 pages typed and double-spaced or legibly handwritten. Electronic submissions are gratefully received.
- Writers may elect to write anonymously or under a pseudonym.
- For references cited in an article, writers should attempt to provide the necessary bibliographic information. Refer to the references cited in past issues for examples.
- Editors look for developed pieces that address topics substantially. Manuscripts go through a preliminary reading and then are sent to review by the Editorial Board. Those that are of suitable interest are returned to the author with comments or suggestions. Editors work with writers on composition and form, and where necessary may help the author with referencing and bibliographic information, not readily available in prisons. Selected articles are returned to authors for their approval before publication. Papers not selected are returned with comments from the editor. Revised papers may be resubmitted.
- Please submit biographical and contact information, to be published alongside articles unless otherwise indicated.

Au *JPP*, nous soutenons le droit des personnes incarcérées à exercer leur liberté d'expression conformément à l'article 2 de la *Charte canadienne des droits et libertés* et enchâssé dans les constitutions nationales ailleurs dans le monde. Nous croyons que la publication des écrits des personnes incarcérées est un outil nécessaire pour faciliter la transparence en milieu carcéral. Nous accueillons les soumissions de tous les prisonniers actuels et anciens, et sommes impatients d'entendre vos commentaires sur les questions mentionnées ci-dessus. Veuillez partager cet avis avec toute personne qui pourrait être intéressée à contribuer à notre revue. Nous demandons à ceux et celles qui choisissent de soumettre une courte notice biographique et de nous faire savoir si vous souhaitez être publié de manière anonyme. Nous sommes impatients d'examiner vos soumissions qui suivent les directives de la revue ci-dessous et espérons avoir de vos nouvelles bientôt.

- Le Journal ne publiera aucun sujet faisant l'apologie de la haine, du sexisme, du racisme, de la violence ou soutenant la peine de mort.
- Le Journal ne publie pas de matériel qui se concentre généralement sur le cas juridique de l'auteur, bien que l'utilisation des expériences personnelles de l'auteur comme illustration d'un sujet plus large soit encouragée.
- Le Journal ne publie généralement pas de fiction et ne publie généralement pas de poésie. Des illustrations, des dessins et des peintures peuvent être soumis comme couvertures potentielles.
- Les articles ne doivent pas dépasser 20 pages dactylographiées et en double interligne ou lisibles à la main. Les soumissions électroniques sont les bienvenues.
- Les auteurs peuvent choisir d'écrire de manière anonyme ou sous un pseudonyme.
- Pour les références citées dans un article, les auteurs doivent s'efforcer de fournir les informations bibliographiques nécessaires. Reportez-vous aux références citées dans les numéros précédents pour des exemples.
- Les éditeurs recherchent des articles développés qui abordent des sujets de manière substantielle. Les manuscrits font l'objet d'une lecture préliminaire, puis sont envoyés pour examen par le comité de rédaction. Ceux qui présentent un intérêt approprié sont renvoyés à l'auteur avec des commentaires ou des suggestions. Les éditeurs travaillent avec les auteurs sur la composition et la forme et, si nécessaire, peuvent aider l'auteur avec des références et des informations bibliographiques, qui ne sont pas facilement disponibles dans les prisons. Les articles sélectionnés sont retournés aux auteurs pour approbation avant publication. Les articles non sélectionnés sont retournés avec les commentaires de l'éditeur. Les articles révisés peuvent être resoumis.
- Veuillez soumettre des informations biographiques et de contact, à publier avec les articles, sauf indication contraire.

IMPORTANT – DATES – IMPORTANTES

Submissions by authors:	1 May |
soumissions par auteurs :	mai 2024

Editorial decision and reviewer comments to authors: 1 July |
décision éditoriale et commentaires aux auteurs :   juillet 2024

Revised manuscripts: 15 October |
manuscripts révisés :   octobre 2024

Final editorial decision to authors: 15 December |
décision éditoriale finale aux auteurs :   décembre 2024

Publication date: 2025
Publication date :   2025

SUBMISSIONS | SOUMISSIONS

Via email to jpp@uottawa.ca or by mail to the address below:

Journal of Prisoners on Prisons
c/o Department of Criminology
University of Ottawa
120 University Private – Room 14049
Ottawa, Ontario, Canada
K1N 6N5

———————

Par email to jpp@uottawa.ca ou par la poste à l'adresse suivante :

Journal of Prisoners on Prisons
c/o Départment de criminologie
University d'Ottawa
120 Université – Salle 14049
Ottawa, Ontario, Canada
K1N 6N5

COVER ART

"End the Prison Industrial Complex" (front cover)
Peter Collins
2011

"i-chain" (back cover)
Peter Collins
2011

Peter Collins was a writer, artist, musician, cartoonist, activist, filmmaker, organizer, and prisoners' rights advocate. Peter was a social critic who offered thoughtful insights about the structures of violence inherent in the world around us. His tireless commitment to social justice from inside prison made him a target of harassment by the Correctional Service of Canada (CSC), which ultimately prevented his release. Peter passed away on 13 August 2015 of bladder cancer after having served 32 years on a Life 25 prison sentence. He was 10 years past his parole eligibility dates.